WATER MARKED
Journal of a Naked Fly Fisherman

by ROBERT LYON

Also by Robert Lyon:
Rivers of Dreams - Orca Books, Editor.

Published by
Water Marked Press
Lopez Island, Washington

Produced by
Paper Jam Publishing
Eastsound, Washington
Book Design by Eileen Anne Dean

Cover photography:
Ruby Mountain—Ken Morrish
Author—Gregg Blomberg Photography

Printed in the United States of America

ISBN 1-888345-14-4

Library of Congress 98-68503

First Edition

To my brother Hal, for his indomitable spirit, his extraordinary ability to engage, his passion for the outdoors, and most of all, his enduring love of me.
I love you too.

Acknowledgments

This is kind of like writing in high school yearbooks on graduation day. I want to thank my friends for helping to make this book possible, for going on these fishing adventures with me, some of them more harebrained than others.

Thanks to my son-in-law, Ken Morrish, for his companionship and his sure camera on the rain waters of the Olympics, the Deschutes, the Middle Fork and the Beaver. That two such inveterates would converge upon two women (our future wives) who did not know one end of a fly rod from another is cosmic humor. To their credit though, Mia Morrish has evolved into a first rate fly fisher, while my wife Pamela developed quickly and retired at the top of her game—a wild steelhead on a fly.

To my first wife Gwen, who endured much as the proverbial "fishing widow." Although as a family we spent many happy nights nestled along the banks of the river when the boys were growing up, her life might have been more rewarded by someone less obsessive than myself. Thank you for putting up with all you did.

To my Dad, and my brother Hal. Although our father did not have the bug as my brother and I did, he took us on some fine adventures into the wilds of Canada, for which I am grateful. Hal is fourteen years older than myself and effectively served as a mentor. By my reckoning, there are essentially three things Hal afforded me. The first is a deep sense of being loved and cherished—very cool. The second is the inspiration for achieving whatever you set your sights on. The list goes on with this guy—West Point to PhD, best selling author to Tony winner—behavior that eventually inspired Hal to write a book on his compulsive over-achieving. The legacy to me, though, was less grandiose. I can get what I go after, it seems, but there is a karmic proviso—objectives must be deeply aligned with my path. The third is a passion for fishing and, recently (long incubation), bird hunting. As a kid there was nothing, absolutely *nothing*, more exciting than *Brother* (as I called him) coming home from West Point on a holiday and taking me fishing. Ironically, while he tends to think of *me* as the master fisherman, it is really Hal who is the anointed. Thanks for your loyalty when times were tough and your support of each small success along the way.

A warm thanks to long time friend, Steve Thomsen. Steve is just as good as a fishing partner gets. I could have called this collection *Shoe-*

string Adventures. My fishing adventures were definitely on a shoe-string when I met Steve in Oregon about 25 years ago. At the time my wife and I had bought our first house and were struggling to make ends meet and raise a couple of young boys. Fishing was compulsion, the Deschutes River a shrine. That I could be paid to take people fishing, or paid to put fishing stories in print made a lot of sense to me; it meant more time on the river. Many of our adventures, especially in the early years when my desire for traveling around Oregon chasing fish out-stripped my ability to pay my share of the expenses, were funded by Steve. He is the ultimate field companion—cheerful, cooperative, mas-ter problem solver (the guy's an engineer), strong, brave and willing to handle the photographic chores. More importantly, he is always the first guy up in the morning to get the coffee going (even serves me the first cup in bed). It was Steve who showed me the white-water ropes on the Deschutes and it was his job as roustabout that I took over when his pregnant wife Joanie neared the end of her term. I plan to return the favor as soon his kids are out of the nest and take Steve on an envelope-pushing, British Columbian, sea kayak, fly fishing odyssey.

Many thanks to Joe Vranizan, starting fullback on the flag football team I coached in 1978 when I worked as a Recreation Director for the City of Portland. Our friendship focused on fishing adventures and Joe became an extremely popular member of our family. Together we explored the Oregon Coast. "Cape Capers" we called our camping trips to the tip (as in tent pitched two feet from edge of cliff) of the state's many fine capes. We drove the old VW bus like it was an off-road vehicle, talking God and the nature of reality and feeling a kind of traveling transcendentalism that the old micro-busses were so condu-cive to. Our signature trip was when the bus was in demand at home or we couldn't afford the gas and dug out the giant two piece hitchhiking sign instead. Gwen would drop us off at the freeway entrance heading east with our rods, reels, waders, camping equipment and that big sign that you could read a hundred yards off.

To the inns and lodges that fed and housed our parties of hungry and exhausted fishermen. Each was selected after careful research and are listed in the side-bars at the end of each article. Thanks for your cooperation.

A thank you to the editors of the different magazines wherein these and other stories originally appeared. The stories didn't always arrive on their desks ready for layout. Inevitably, they were twice as long as they had contracted for. In particular, my thanks to Silvio Calabi and Jim Barnett at *Fly Rod & Reel*, and Frank Amato at *STS* for publishing my first story. And thank you Eileen, for producing this book and for your patience with me.

A special thanks to Tom Barnett up at Ross Lake Resort for his continued friendship and generosity over the years. A guy could spend a lifetime checking out the lake and surrounding wilderness. To Donna Troutman at Deschutes U-Boats for her carte blanche support with boats and equipment for use on the Deschutes River, year after year. Deschutes U-Boats generously donated use of their rafts and equipment (including boater's passes and, ice, even) to the Lopez Kid's Summer Workshop Program when it ran the river for a week last summer. Many thanks from the kids and staff.

I am grateful to the outfitters and guides who donated energy and time to host their home waters. Gary and Kitty Shelton and Eric Rector of Middle Fork River Outfitters in Idaho, whose stewardship of the Middle Fork River is as much a service to the environment as it is to their valued customers. To Dave Steinbaugh of Waters West. Besides having an engaging streamside manner, the guy is a master of at least three things—rowing a drift boat, fishing a Spey rod and tying a fly. And to Nick Pallis of Angler's Fly Fishing Guide Service for a fine day on the Yakima "messin' about in boats."

Thanks to Ray Pelland, designer of the Kingfisher series of kickboats. From many years experience, I believe that these are the ultimate in a personal-sized fishing boat. Ray has been generous with his prodigy and we've run them on many rivers throughout the Northwest. In the higher class of rapids, the effect is empowering; what you lack in sheer size, you make up for in maneuverability. If you can figure a route, you can probably negotiate it. The boats are truly the Porsche of the rafting world.

A thank you to Dave Hadden on Vancouver Island, for his stewardship of wild fish in the Campbell River area, and his stewardship of me, in particular, when I arrived broke as a stick a few years back. A special thanks to the crews of the lighthouses along the island's wild outer coast, especially the Carmanah and Cape Beale Lights. Sadly, these keepers are currently being replaced by automated lights, another sad testimony to the techno tit we badly need weaning from.

Finally, my deepest appreciation of my wife Pamela for her companionship on several of these adventures, her artistic photographic contribution, her understanding and willingness to support my dreams, and to her unflinchingly high standards, which somehow and occasionally I manage to meet.

This collection of stories is essentially a celebration of fly fishing and, tacitly, both the places and the adventures that fishing affords us. I have provided full-length side-bars, a la journal style, at the end of most selections to encourage readers to take off on an adventure of their own. To take this one step further, I'll say this—it is one thing to muster the drive to undertake a fishing adventure for ourselves, another to share one in print with interested parties, but yet another to pick up a kid or three and physically transport them to the river. As the world becomes a smaller and smaller place, this becomes an increasingly important thing to do. Living on an island as I do, it's problematic for the kids to get a taste for the rivers of the desert, the streams and lakes of the mountains and it remains on the shoulders of both the parents and adults in the community to make a point of taking the kids to such places.

On our island we are fortunate to have Celia Snapp, human tornado and director of the Lopez Kid's Summer Workshop Program. Celia has categorically inventoried the pool of local outdoor talent and set up a program to tap it. Her summer program effectively offers our kids a viable opportunity to hike or fish, sail or kayak, camp and bike within our diverse bioregion. Joe Vranizan and I got involved in this and took a bunch of kids on a week-long fly fishing expedition down the Deschutes. Those of us living in cities are surrounded by a sea of a different sort. It is no less difficult for a family from Pittsburgh or San Francisco to make a pilgrimage to the nearby mountains or rivers, than it is for us. Remember the generations to come. Take a kid someplace cool.

Photo by Gregg Blomberg Photography.

Author with Matthew Sutton, working on casting fundementals before the trip.

Portraits of a fisherman as a boy.
Bottom left, dad, brother and cousin with a string of very small fish.

Hardcore hitch-hiking, the shoe-string approach. Joe Vranizan and myself.

Pamela's first, and last, catch and release.

Circling Orcas Island.

Ray Pelland and a fleet of his Wunderboats in action.

Steve Thomsen tailing a big cutthroat on Megin Lake in the B.C. wilderness.

Joe Vranizan, early years, Deschutes.

Foreword

My wife Pamela actually suggested the title of this book, pointing out my passion for water, not just as it pertains to fishing, but in the roles that water has served me over the years. And she's right. It has been my preoccupation, my occupation, my home (first a houseboat, now on a little island in Puget Sound), and, in recent years, the milieu of my most intensely water-borne experiences to date.

I cannot remember the first time I fished; it was Germany at the age of five or six, I believe. It didn't require much of an incubation period either. As for fly fishing, the focus of this collection, I was initiated at the age of eight by a friend of my father's, a sports writer from the *Washington Post*. We left the D.C. suburbs in the predawn darkness, heading deep into the Adirondack Mountains. I could hardly see over the dash of his stately Buick as we followed our headlights east, parking some hours later at a pull-off alongside a deeply forested road. Below the highway the ground dropped steeply away; a forest canopy towered overhead. We made our way into the valley below and found a stream, much like a string of pearls, a series of pools connected by riffles tumbling down the mountain. My mentor showed me how to sneak up to the tail of each pool from the head of the one below and, standing in shorts in the icy water (I didn't notice), I would toss my little dry up onto the surface of the pool ahead where the magic would take place. I caught several beautiful trout that day and soaked up the experience like a sponge. It was provocative fishing for a little guy with a predilection for such things, and in my soul the act of fishing with a fly was stamped that day. While fishing has always been the meat of my relationship with water, the marking business went deeper.

It was the winter of '51, as best as I can recall, on a small troop transport ship crossing the North Atlantic Ocean from New York to Germany via the British Isles. I was about four at the time and the weather was a mixed bag, from blue skies and endless blue seas with white combers curling at the crests, whales in the distance and porpoises playing in the bow wake, to legendary North Atlantic gales. Being on the open ocean in the best of weather was heady stuff for a little guy; riding the back of a bucking tempest was an experience beyond my wildest dreams. It was during one of several such storms—surrounded by enormous, heaving, steely gray seas and a marauding nickel

Coke machine that busted loose from its moorings in the rec room—that I found religion.

In a word, it was awesome. A potent cocktail of one part terror and three parts awe (a tasty brew). Since that day I have been drawn, inexorably, to water. While fishing has unquestionably been the leitmotif of this relationship (as witnessed in the following pages), there has been a steady, sure progression from chattering Black Forest stream, to Adirondack creek, from farmer's ponds to mountain lakes to one rambunctious river in the Oregon desert where, in a kind of marriage, I committed fully to my passion.

After several years on that Oregon river, guiding fly fishermen and running rapids in a McKenzie dory, I felt that I was ready to move on. There was no question as to where, either. North and west, closer to the edge of civilization, closer to the Mother sea. Interestingly, while I still lived in Oregon, Joe Vranizan and I took a long hike down the West Coast Trail on Vancouver Island's southwestern coast. As we slogged along a muddy trail with sixty-pound packs, I found my eyes glancing continually to the sea. It hit me then. It was not enough to hike along the coast with a fine view to the west; the old cocktail was calling again, begging to be slugged down. I moved to the San Juan Islands, thinking that was close enough and, to get my feet wet, rowed a little seven foot raft around Orcas Island. But, before long, the surrounding inland sea seemed as bucolic as the rural island landscape.

The Northwest coast is largely the western shore of large islands—Vancouver Island, and both the Queen Charlotte Archipelago and the Alexander Archipelago of Alaska. When I met Pamela, she had been paddling on the western shores of Vancouver Island for ten years already. She had even built a replica Hooper Bay sealing canoe and paddled it for weeks at a time in this ocean wilderness. I was invited along with Pamela, Gregg Blomberg and Irene Skyriver, and several others on one of these annual month-long outings and haven't been the same since.

Next spring I'm off to circle the Charlottes and spend a couple of months exploring the "highest energy coastline in North America." Of course, I'll have a couple of fly rods along and a passel of tackle; it's one thing to be alone in such an exquisite, intensely energetic environment, but to fly fish there is icing on the cake.

While the majority of these stories focus on fishing, the last of the bunch speaks most pointedly to the title of this book. It is a story of a long, solo kayak odyssey, and the objective is clearly more than fishing. In the course of 102 days traveling alone at sea there were many exceptional opportunities to fish. No matter how extraordinary though, fishing assumes a quality of exalted pragmaticality on such a journey. There is a subsistence rationale at work that smacks of purpose. The need to repeatedly catch and release subsumes to a larger field of excitement. There are exceptions, to be sure, like your first few salmon or casting a three weight from the beach to a school of spanking bluebacks.

In other words, what you have here are "stories of a transcendental fly fisherman;" that could well have been the title of the collection. Fishing has not remained a static act, but has increasingly drawn me to a deeper theater and, ultimately, to the ocean. I think the reason I have not remained in the contented ranks of fraternal fly fishermen and instead have followed the magic to the sea is because of my experience at sea as a child.

My relationship with water has been a benefic thing. I have been fortunate to fish some fine bodies and filaments of water, able to guide on a *solar-system-class* river, to live on a nourishing little island surrounded by a gentle sea and to pay some bills by sharing my adventures in print. There is a parallel, I believe, between finding peace alone in a small boat on an open sea and finding God. Sea is to Mind. "Ride your horse the direction it is going" is a favorite adage of Oriental wisdom, and there has been no doubt all along where my horse was heading.

Enjoy.

Ross Lake
North Cascades
Halloween, 1998

Tigers of the Lower

*Deschutes/August 29th - Kloan.
Haven't touched a steelhead in two
days. One of the fellows in Gordy's
boat wanted to switch over to trout
today and Gordy told him: 'Don't
shoot rabbits on a tiger hunt.' Zen river
wisdom, to be sure. On the sentient
plane or a steelhead expedition, it is
the same good advice.*

from my journal, 1980s.

Appeared originally in variation in *Steelhead Fly Fishing Journal*,
titled, "Deschutes"

 ̤a Cola thermometer nailed under the market awning
 ̣d 106 degrees. The colorful rafting town of Maupin, Or-
 ̣, (pop. 450) is the hub of the river, take-out destination for
 ̣eople floating the upper canyon, access point for the busy stretch
of rapids bordering either side of town for six or seven miles, and
the staging area for guides, shuttles, and fishermen preparing to
float the lower canyons in pursuit of steelhead. After stopping in
town to top off our provisions, we crossed a concrete bridge curving high over the Deschutes and pulled up in front of "The Oasis" for a last minute fix of burgers and frosted shakes. Afterward, we drove a stone's throw north to meet up with lovely Donna
Troutman, of Deschutes U-Boats. Donna has outfitted most of
our trips along the river in the last decade and makes the logistics
of messing with boats and shuttles about as painless as pie.

Our party consisted of Steve Braun—tall, athletic, irrepressible, and one of two civil engineers along on this trip—an easy
going, laconic Pat McDonald, who owned a construction company on Orcas Island where the three of us lived and Steve
Thomsen, the other engineer and old friend of mine, who lives in
the foothills of the North Cascades. Steve is an old hand on the
river and taught me the ropes here years ago. Pat had fished steelhead here before. Steve Braun was the only newcomer to the river.
We had driven south together from our homes in the northern
part of Washington state to float the lower Deschutes and try our
luck at summers.

We decided to haul the rafts inflated to save time and tossed
them on the roof of the truck. The effect was impressive, increasing the height of the rig by another six feet. At the top, we
nested in the rowing frames and tossed up a couple of coolers
packed with ice. We felt a little like the Hindenberg, motoring
slowly down the long access road to our launch point at road's

end. Meanwhile, it was still sweltering at six in the evening and the road was potholed and washboarded and dusty as hell, but the river running beside the road gave good cause for heart. It was a mysterious snowy green color; you couldn't see more than five or six feet into it—all a steelie needed to get after your fly. Where it riffled over shallows or twisted around rocks, it was white as new tennis shoes and easy on the eye. We had Bob Marley on the box, and that helped. By the time we were half way along, there were shadows on the water. We had to decide between fishing around the campground that evening and camping there that night, or getting on the water and maybe missing the evening fish.

The road swung back on itself and dropped down into the big barren campground near the mouth of Mack's Canyon. This was take-out for the relatively short but productive stretch of water to the south and launch point for boats heading down the final twenty-eight miles to the Columbia. It was also a base of operations for the jet boats, or "sleds," as they're called, that could run in either direction. We pulled up at the boat launch, tumbled out of the gondola and began the transfer of equipment, having finally decided to leave civilization behind sooner than later.

We hurried to empty out the truck and get the boats in order, still hoping to have a shot at wetting a line that night. Much later than we had hoped, though, we pushed the boats off from the beach. I spun the boat in a tight circle, getting in synch with the oars. *God, it felt good to be back on the water!*

It was getting on toward dusk and we figured we'd be lucky to find a decent camp—forget about fishing. Ahead of us the river broke up into gray gravel bars and thin, green islands. The first of the churning rapids splashed water over the side like a priest's blessing as deep shadows darkened the Canyon. We could hear chukar calling along shore, the metallic whine of nighthawks slashing through the darkling corridor overhead, and the flute-like trill of canyon wrens from the cliff towering above the deep bend in the river we were floating through.

We settled on a mediocre camp on mediocre water that night, and would have to wait till morning to fish; it was getting too dark to do much else. An old black-powder storage building stood in shadows on the flat; I had made the mistake of taking shelter there one night years ago to escape fifty-mile-per-hour winds. It was a wild place to crash. The cobbled rock wall around my bed were scorpion and black widow condos for sure. It was snakey looking too, but it was the train that iced the cake. The train track curves by within spitting distance (I hadn't realized this in the dark) and I popped up like a jack-in-the-box that night when the train came along. Its enormous halide light transformed night into day. The shadows playing against the cliff across the river were phantasmagorical, and the deafening rumble of its passing rattled the old foundation.

The wind screamed through our little scruff camp that night; a stack of paper plates feathered off the folding kitchen table, the four of us madly chasing after them with flashlights. We'd gotten in at dark and hadn't unpacked much but the essentials. Our gear lay like an enormous shell game; *anything* could be in *any one* of fifteen river bags and boxes strewn around the flat. None of us were in the best of moods as we sat stoically in the dark in folding chairs along the cobbled riverbed sipping gin and seltzers before throwing out our pads among the sagebrush. First nights in the canyon can be problematic.

Morning, though, is another story altogether. It is an exquisite time in a desert, especially the half-light of a river canyon. The air is cool and smells of river and sage and dry grass and there is no wind. There's something, too, about how the soul disengages each night like a clutch, letting you shift into your new environs upon waking.

Sure enough, we were fired up the next morning and much happier campers than the night before. Ahead of us lay twenty-eight miles of some of the finest fly water in the world. No ordinary stretch of river either, but water flowing over staircased basalt, with spires and ledges and sunken troughs. Like fishing a river flowing over the tumbled marble of the Parthenon, like fishing over the sunken tombs of Ideath. We fished through the fast, broken water in front of camp a couple of times and came up empty, then threw everything aboard the boats and pushed off. Leap-frogging around each other, we fished our way north, hoping to sample as many shady stretches of water as we could before the sun torched the canyon bottom. We covered some sweet looking water and pretty much had the place to ourselves. To no avail though, as we had not the slightest touch between the three of us. Lounging aboard the big raft with our waders rolled down and iced sodas in our hands, we had no concern with rapids; they were all waiting within the final seven miles. We passed two other groups of rafters that day and one stolid looking jet boat captain who returned our open-palmed gesture with an empty shake of his head.

The east wall of the canyon was lit up in lovely pastel—pinks, yellows, mauves. I rebuilt my leader while Braun ran the boat, wetting each blood-knot and snugging it tight. Around a deep S-bend the river swirled through an enormous, sunken boulder field off the east bank. We stood up floating over, squinting down through milky shafts of light, but the channel was too deep and swirly to see anything. It was exciting water nonetheless, and had rarely failed to yield a steelhead or two each time I'd fished it through. We pulled in several hundred yards below and set up camp in the mottled shade of a stand of alders.

Desert sun beat mercilessly into the canyon that afternoon and kept most of us under the trees. Braun sunned happily in the buff

Photo by Ken Morrish

In my element—cool water piling against my back, hot sun on bare shoulders, anticipating a strike at any moment.

Three amigos *halfway down the access road to launch at Mack's Canyon.*

Photo by Steve Thomsen

Author, Pat, Steve. A honeydew moment.

Photo by Steve Thomsen

on a lounge chair by the water, greeting the occasional passing boats with a wave. *For an engineer*, I thought, *the guy has tremendous cool.*

The wind picked up and blew strong that evening but we were determined to try to find some fish. On the Deschutes, you put your eggs in two baskets—morning and evening. Deschutes fish shun direct sun but rise freely under cloudy skies or in secondary light. Steve and Pat had hiked downriver to explore the Bull Run water. Now Braun and I stood together in the camp kitchen, watching the line of approaching shade inch down the canyon wall, eating out of a bag of salsa chips, and scooping big loads of ice-cold salsa out of a plastic tub. I filled a pair of Ziplocks with fresh water and slipped them into the back of my vest, then grabbed a pair of PowerBars and threw them in too. We struck out across the rocky slope behind camp and climbed to the old railroad grade still soaking up sun a hundred feet above the river.

After a short hike we scrambled down a slope full of boulders so hot you couldn't touch them. We could see currents of cold, gray-green water swirling through an enormous amount of rock blasted from the cliff side in the early 1900s, courtesy of Jim Hill and the Burlington Northern. It was extremely fishy looking. Getting around on shore or just down from the grade, though, was a bitch.

Huge shards of basalt made the wading dicey too, but we weren't complaining; it made supreme holding water for the steelhead. The run is about fifty yards long, and to fish it thoroughly you had to find your way among the sunken casting stations. With the brisk current and the boulders, the surface was a roiling boil. This made an intricate relationship between the positioning of a fisherman and the swim of his fly. After you were finished with a particular piece of the run, or beat, you reeled in, tightened your wading belt and bobbed your way to the next. Mid-day, with a pair of high-contrast glasses, you could make out a route of sorts between deep channels and rock, but wading without direct sunlight was a crap shoot; to reach the furthest stations, you typically ended up swimming.

The wind busted upriver, forcing us to turn our backs and huddle protectively against the worst blows; the surface fritz made it nearly impossible to see underwater. I had fished my way into the middle of the run (with a foot of water inside my waders), standing ankle deep on a boulder the size of a Volkswagen, when I found what I was after.

It took at the end of a long double haul where I fed additional line into the drift to reach a distant lie, then it rolled like a lake trout on the surface for a few moments before it swam hard downriver. A moment later a distant sploosh of water marked where the big fish had dived free; I nearly made a sploosh of my own backward off the rock from the sudden release. I reeled in and found that it had thrown the hook, at least, and not broken off. We fished into twilight without another bump, squatting on our rock perches to gather remaining light. *It's funny,* I thought, as I made my way back to shore, *the change that comes over you with the dwindling light.* I was reminded of Nick Adams and his fear of the swamp, where "...in the fast deep water, in the half light, the fishing would be tragic...." Without the sun the river is a hammered veneer, a visually impenetrable dimension of surface only, while the bulk of the river itself, hidden beneath, appears dark and ominous. We retrieved two cold beers Braun had stashed in the river and scrambled up the slope to the grade, happy to be kicking up dust.

The influx of people and industry to the canyon began with the Oregon Trail. With the Trail came ferries and ferry men, ranchers grazing their cattle along the river banks and speculative farmers casting an eye up and down the choicest sections of the canyon floor, thinking: *Now I just bet I could make this land work.*

Just after the turn of the century not one but *two* competing railroads forced their way through the entire length of canyon. These would be Edward Harriman's Union Pacific and Jim "The Empire Builder" Hill's Great Northern. In what was billed as the last great railroad race, thousands of East Europeans laborers using dangerous black powder (just before the development of dynamite), chiseled, picked, hand-drilled, and blasted their way up a canyon once thought impassable.

When the railroad was finally pushed through, another wave of people swept in. Mines and stage stations, supply depots and inns, tollbridges and general stores sprang up. Townships were formed. Water for irrigation and consumption drew down the water table. The riparian zone was given over to sheep and cattle. Waste was returned to the river. The balanced ecosystem of the river canyon began to tip.

Pelton Reregulating Dam, installed in 1958, did just that— 're-regulated'. With the coming of the dam, gone was the pattern of natural river flow, the periods of extreme high flow that hydrated the surrounding plains, flushed sediment from spawning beds and recruited fresh gravel. And as a result of the dam, the Deschutes is now, 40 years later, about six degrees warmer in summer. With record high 1998 temperatures in Oregon, the White River, a tributrary draining the glaciated slopes of Mount Hood, kept the Deschutes in spate virtually throughout the season. Furthermore, steelhead that typically begin entering the Deschutes in mid to late July, largely remained in the Columbia River well into September. Even before the White kicked in, turning the river a coffee brown, the water temperature in the Deschutes was just too hot, apparently, for fish to want to enter.

On the upside, there has been considerable energy invested in both the conservation and management of the river canyon. Sounding like an English teacher's worst nightmare, Congress used the phrase *'outstandingly remarkable'* to describe the relative value of the resources existing here. When Congress designated the lower hundred miles of the Deschutes River Canyon a "National Wild and Scenic River" in 1988, it legislated the opportunity to consciously manage the river's future.

Decades of over-grazing and aggressive agri-practices have left the critical riparian zone in a less-than-healthy condition. With recreational use accelerating over the last twenty years, human impact has been greater than ever before. It is the narrow green corridor along the river bank that is hit hardest by boaters, and it is precisely this zone that aquatic insects, the fish that feed on them, nesting birds, and even big game require for survival.

We may never see the return of the great Roosevelt elk once found in the canyon, or the antelope and big horn sheep that lived in the Mutton Mountains, but we can walk lightly when we visit the river, inform ourselves on environmental issues by reading the brochures, pamphlets, and newsletters (which are very well done, incidentally) distributed by the managing agencies, and we can certainly bring along our best common sense.

Bryan Cunningham was involved with the technical aspects of the river's management plan. When I spoke with him, he said that of all the values that surfaced when the Deschutes was under consideration for protection, "fisheries" rose right to the top of the list. Indeed, the lower river is commonly considered to be the best summer steelhead, dry line river in the world. While that may seem like a highly qualified, even esoteric, designation, in my mind it is speaking to the heart of the fly fishing experience itself.

Dry lines, or floating lines, are the ones that come to mind

Photo by Author on Fujifilm

Camp along the lower river.

Photo by Ken Morrish

*Steve Thomsen and myself standing in the middle of the river,
fishing "the ledges." It was a hot day.*

Photo by Author on Fujifilm

Chowline.

Photo by Steve Thomsen

Bigger than average Deschutes steelhead.

when we think of fly fishing as art; light and arabesque, they are a pleasure to cast. "Summers" are the steelhead that come along when we can relax and settle into a rhythm of river camps and balmy nights and fishing sessions at the crack of dawn and at dusk. There are typically large numbers of fish in the river from late July through November.

The lower—the words still conjure up a halcyon netherworld of midnight camps and dawn patrols. Maybe it's the semi-delirious state produced by sleep deprivation and the occasional maniacal fishing that are the chief ingredients. It isn't always wild and halcyon either; much of the time it is frustration and disappointment and digging deep to learn lessons that are not just about fishing. Throw in liberal amounts of fatigue and pain from sheer exposure, and throw in a lonely moonscape countryside. Throw in friends, plenty of delicious food and iced beer.

When I worked here, we would spend nearly half of each year in the canyon, sleeping under the stars. We were always eager to get on the river in the spring because we'd been gone all winter. The pace of a trout fishing expedition along the upper river is a leisurely forty-something-mile stretch. Up with the sun and, after a substantial breakfast and basking period, we would take to the water for the banker's-hour may-fly hatch. Fishing our way downriver with delicious deli lunches on shaded islands, then more fishing until we arrived in camp. But after a couple of months on the upper river hunting *rabbits*—and a marvellous stretch of river it is—our thoughts would turn inexorably to *tigers* and *the lower*.

Feeling more like an infantry platoon sometimes, rather than a camp full of fishermen, we would be up in the dark just before dawn, drinking huge pots of coffee and hungrily downing sweet pastries and melons and making plans. Then we were off to secure our runs on the water surrounding camp before the jet boats had enough light to negotiate the rapids. Or sometimes we drifted in the dark along a stretch of river that we knew intimately and we were the first rods through a favorite run a mile below camp.

These were powerful fishing hours from first light until the sun tipped the canyon wall. Sometimes we would fish the water we started in over and over again if the fish were striking. Other times we might fish through six or seven different pieces until we found fish. And other times, of course, we'd come up empty handed. With the coming of the sun, our efforts would gradually taper off—lunch swims and espresso were in order, or catnaps, or maybe we were the boat designated to secure camp and we would float downstream drinking iced fluids and diving overboard to cool off.

Fishing the Deschutes is definitely a split-shift operation. Morning fish - afternoon *siesta*. Evening fish - night *siesta*. Repeated four or five days at a stretch, it takes a toll. There is never quite enough sleep, in the summer at least, and the hypnotic residue of altered consciousness becomes a way of life.

Pat and Steve came up empty fishing the long, gently curving shoreline below camp. I had fished that particular stretch very little but suspected it held secrets of its own. For dinner that night we had Pat's enormous, venison-tasting, home-grown, grass-fed steaks. Pat was a great guy to have along on a trip like this. Not only comfortable and easy to be around, he was an excellent fisherman and was quick to help out with chores around camp; there was no trace of the nose-to-the-grindstone-businessman here. *For a high powered contractor,* I thought, *the guy certainly knew how to switch gears.* We huddled together playing poker in our copse of trees, listening to the music of the hissing lanterns, the river, the wind, and the occasional passing train. The inverted lid of an 86-quart cooler neatly kept our cards from scattering like the first night's plates, and the wind, at least, kept the swarming caddis at bay. Mosquitoes are rare here but the clouds of caddis drawn to lights at night are nearly as bothersome.

One of the most difficult aspects of successfully fishing the Deschutes is making the right call on the morning slot. With only a couple of hours of fishing time before the sun hits the water, you either fish around camp or pack up in the dark and fish your way down river as you go. It is far easier, unless you are traveling with support, to plan on fishing camp water thoroughly, then dropping leisurely with the sun. We decided to do just that the next day.

Steve Thomsen caught and released our *first* fish of the trip, and the only fish we saw that morning. It was a slow running, dogging fish that didn't jump at all.

"It was a wild fish, too," he told us later. "A big, bright buck. About nine pounds I'd guess." It was funny like that, the difference in individual fish. Some would smoke you—hatchery or wild, big or small—while others would play a lackluster game of tug-of-war—*not a lot different from people*, I thought.

By noon we had loaded the boats with a noticeable increase in order and pushed off. The river wound through enormous arid, hillocks under an ennervating desert sun. The bunch and cheat grasses covering the hillsides were dry and thirsting for the meager fall rain. *You wouldn't catch me here without this river.* The faintest rumbling sound caught our attention; it appeared to be coming from down river. Deeper than the roar of the sleds, it was the tell-tale arrival of the train.

The leitmotif of the canyon are the green and black engines of the Burlington Northern line. They reappear several times each day and tie it all together for me. Whether I'm sweating a difficult rapid, high as a kite with a buck steelie on the end of my line, or a little down from several days of screwing the pooch, the train is like a touchstone. Using a kind of energetic empathy, I recharge from its thunderous horsepower as it passes by. As a symbol of human diligence, of the thousands of man hours of back breaking work it took to lay track by hand in this rugged place, it puts my own successes and frustrations into perspective and acts to center and balance me. I don't know exactly what it is—maybe I was a worker here in the canyon in my last life—but during the days I worked here I was haunted by the history of the railroad days. I explored dilapidated railroad trestles and old rock ovens, still standing like giant beehives with their single keystone at the top, and hiked rock-buttressed wagon roads leading down onto broad flats along the river where the great white-tented enclaves were pitched. Most poignantly, I would sit a moment to rest when I was at the end of my own rope, weary from little sleep and too much work—that's when I could best identify with a Hungarian immigrant sitting on a rock (maybe even the same rock) in a dull torpor on a rare day off. It was all *extremely* evocative to me. So evocative, in fact, I spent a winter writing a five-hundred-page historical novel set here at that time.

Looking industrious in the early light and carrying lumber and Indian hoboes hunkering in open boxcars (waving at us and us at them), the train filled the narrow canyon that morning with its presence . . . *rakata-rakata-rakata-rakata*. Weathered, flat-topped trees reminiscent of African savannah were scattered along the water's edge, black and white cattle were sprinkled like salt and pepper over the yellow hills. The river bent in a lazy half-circle around a broad flat and our camp, which we could just then see was vacant, lay immediately ahead. We named this camp the Park Camp years ago because it was like an oasis with its short green grass and border of shade alder trees. Cattle are excellent lawn mowers. When the lower river was put into a preservation trust for the public, though, the riparian zone was fenced off.

Photo by Author on Fujifilm

Native man dip-net fishing for salmon at Shearer's Falls.

Photo by Eric Lyon

*The Pacific Rattlesnake—a very large specimen.
Will usually see one or two each trip.*

The release of shrubs attested to the returning health of this shore-line ecosystem, but I confess to a recidivistic yearning for that well manicured camp of old. Besides, I liked the cows wandering through our camp at night like large, nocturnal dogs.

Encamped in the most remote section of country for miles and miles around, we were hoping we might all get into some fish that evening and make the decision to lay over another day an easy one. There was plenty of excellent water around camp. The Steves hiked downriver to fish the bend and the sumptuous False Tail Pool and all the pockets in between. Pat rowed across the river to fish the runs and holes I had shown him by wading out in front of camp and pointing with my finger. I probably should have gone across with him; it was exceptionally difficult water to see, even when you were right on top of it. I had discovered most of it while working here as a roustabout, when I would have plenty of time to fish after my kitchen chores were done. Prime water was taken by clients, and I would finish up the dishes and hike well out of camp to explore on my own. I made a wealth of discoveries that summer, not just about these particular hot spots directly across the river, but about the essence of such water and how to read it elsewhere. Selfishly, though, I hiked upstream alone that evening to visit the flats.

It was hot, damned hot still, hiking in waders in bright sunlight along the old hard-pan railroad grade. It took an effort to hike the distance in waders, especially in the sun. Half an hour later I came around a bend and glanced upriver. I was disappointed to discover two fishermen already in the run I had hoped to fish. Hiking a little further, I ducked under the cattle fence and bushwhacked through a forest of blackberry and sumac growing in the delta of a side canyon. The blackberries had peaked early, leaving me hungering for their bloody sweetness. Standing on shore, I could see a drift boat pulled in at the Steelie Flats camp.

A folding table stuck out the back, though, a ray of hope. *If they hadn't unpacked yet,* I figured, *they might not be intending to stay.*

The flats were a symphony. Steelie Flats we called 'em, a complex melody of gentle, dovetailing tones, while the run I was heading to immediately below was a cacophony more like *Wipe-out,* the old surfer instrumental. I touched up my flies and picked out a wind knot, glancing up river every so often to check on my neighbors. I enjoyed the fast riffling bend I was working through. It was like *zip, zip, zip,* as your casts whipped over the narrow seam. Dear little space existed that a fish would want to hold in along this outer bank, but a knife-like seam remained along the edge where they would invariably move. Moreover, it was such stimulating water to fish, feeling it pushing against you and the sound of it curling and splashing against itself. And when you hooked a fish here—my *god*—it was gone like a bullet. Swimming upriver in the swift, broken water was not an option; instead they shot downriver with the fast currents in a physical, bucking, screaming, *into-your-backing-in-about-six-seconds* kind of run. My favorite!

But it was not to be that day. By the time I'd worked my run to the bottom, though, the fellows above me had packed up and floated on. *Good news,* I figured, as I hiked on up, *is I have the flats to myself—bad news is there don't look to be many fish around.* They'd missed some of the best casting stations aboard the deeper rocks though; I took solace in that.

I hiked upriver, waded out to a submerged rock, and sat down to let the water rest. I rested myself at the same time and took out my pipe to keep me company. The flats were like a sheet of dimpled glass; anomalies in the current betrayed only the largest boulders. Never quite broken, the river rolled like a slow sheet of simmering oil in the second-hand light of the canyon. The run was the size of a football field, and I fished it that evening with full, long swings, working easily down through the gentle water, the track of my fly across the flats like the tiniest scurrying shrew. There were no seams to concentrate anticipation, only the gentle marring of the boils.

The sky was beginning to draw color when I reached the tail. It was fine water all right. Although I came through without a touch, it had been a pleasure to fish. I swear, it's hard to lose out here; like sex without the finale, a guy didn't need many fish to be satisfied when he was swinging flies through water like this! As I waded back to shore from the furthest station I could see someone entering the river a couple of hundred yards below me; it looked like Pat. As I reached shore I saw his rod go up and heard the faintest whoop. But then, just as quick, he was casting again.

On the way back to camp I found myself remembering what I'd heard about the river that season. Marty Sherman wrote saying that he'd floated once earlier that summer and was relegating the rest of the season to fishing Alaska instead. The water was extremely low and returns were expected to be well below average. We had had little choice anyway, setting the logistical machinery of organizing a float trip in motion from four hundred miles away.

We had our chairs in a half-circle beside the river with the wind rattling overhead. Plenty of sunburned heads and necks and faces showed in the group as we sat along the bank sipping gin and tonics or cold beers in the yellow, hissing light of our swaying gas lantern. I couldn't remember the last time we'd had so many long line releases. We must have hooked half a dozen fish between the three of us in several days of fishing, but had landed only the one. Pat's fish, below me that evening, remained true to

The Sheik.

Photo by Steve Thomsen

Italian rock oven - Circa 1909

Photo by Steve Thomsen

Bucking the big wave at Colorado.

Photo by Richard Ward

The author taking a moment to connect.
There are some challenging rapids on the river.

Photo by Pamela Maresten

form; a thrown hook for no apparent reason. In the light of his head lamp Pat was working on a couple of wind knots in his leader. Steve again had a fish on for a second or two but couldn't stay with it.

"Has everyone been touching up their points?" I tossed out to the group. The basics would kill you if you overlooked them. Wind knots, dull hooks and tight drag settings were the favorite mistakes. When you had the tip of a hook in a bony mouth for half a second it either caught or slid free. Sharp points made all the difference and we'd check them on the back of our nails to see if they dug in or skipped. By the end of the season my left thumb nail always looked pretty chewed up.

We decided to pack up before first light and fish our way down river in the dark. As much as we would have liked to lay over another night and not have to go through the grind of breaking camp again, we decided our best chance lay in fresh water down stream. I woke in the dark to the alarm beeping insistently on my wrist: 3:30 a.m. We managed a breakfast of fruit, pastry and coffee while we rolled up our bags, loaded the boats, and prowled around with flashlights for anything else. The air was cool over the water as we floated; for a change, there wasn't a breath of wind. A covey of chukar called from a sagebrush gulley. *I want to get down again this fall,* I thought, *and chase those birds around the canyon.* The big bend below camp had good water on both sides. Steve and Pat fished down through the bottom of it and found a pair of fish in a pocket on the east bank.

Steve struck first, an average-sized steelhead of about seven pounds. It was a hatchery fish, our only one landed that trip, with both a ventral fin and an adipose clipped; he killed and dressed it and put it on ice for dinner. We never saw the other. Pat hooked it very close to the bank above the sunken boulders along the outside of the bend. It came off the bottom in at least twelve to fifteen feet of water to exchange the fly for a sudden boil. Then it went deep to center channel and swam hard, straight up river. The drag on a big belly of floating line was tremendous and finally snapped the eight-pound tippet. From across the river, we shared in the excitement; good thing too, as we came up zip. *Steelhead appear by the grace of God,* I reminded myself, *and disappear the same way.*

By Harris Canyon the sun was searching for us in earnest. A lone jet boat passed by. We decided to pass on exploring the petroglyphs up a side canyon nearby and float straight into Corchys. Steve and Pat pulled ashore on the gravel bar there and would try their luck in direct sun. Ducking under a particularly towering bluff, Braun and I ferried into the lingering shade of the western palisades for a final try. While Braun worked over his leader, I waded out to test the water.

"All right, Bob," he said, slyly, "show a virgin how it's done."

"I'll see what I can do."

The water was deepish and flowed along nearly faster than I liked, but hanging by the raft I worked out line a pull at a time and threw it straight out from shore. The currents were so quick it was hard to keep my flies from skittering across the surface. A burst of line shot from my reel. There was a frothing of water not far downstream, then suddenly it was over. *All right,* I thought, *there's fish around.*

"Seemed painless enough," Braun called out, with a laugh.

"You'll get to like it," I said, as I shortened up and started in again. "Trick is not to lose it prematurely."

After several casts I felt another pluck; involuntarily I lifted on the rod. Nothing. I let it back down a moment, peeved with myself for being jumpy. With the fly hanging motionless in the current, the fish actually nipped it again, this time hooking itself in the process. It jumped immediately, a gorgeous fish, bright and pug-nosed and evidently strong. I maneuvered it beside me after an exhaustive give-and-take but missed on my first attempt at tailing. Again I brought it toward me and when I thought I couldn't miss, I slipped my hand tightly around the wrist of its tail. With an explosive wriggle, it shot from my grip and swam between my legs. My rod followed the fish and flipped me flat on my back! *This fish knows judo.* I laughed.

Somehow the steelhead remained on; feeling both foolish and tenacious, I stayed with the fish until, finally, I tailed it. When I turned around, I saw Braun laughing and pointing his camera at me from the boat; I could hear the motor drive pushing the frames.

"Got it all," he said, with a grin.

A jet-boat driver we passed said it was raining like hell in Portland and heading our way. About noon we caught sight of the old bridge abutments strewn across the river in Freebridge. Half a mile further we found our camp, a small but comfortable shelter nestled against an inhospitable shore. We made our rounds in Kloan that evening, fishing extremely hard, but were disappointed to draw a goose egg all around.

We grilled Steve's hatchery fish for dinner that night. Pesto and fresh squeezed lime set it off nicely. With a bottle of good island chardonnay that Pat had brought along for such an occassion, we toasted the spirit of the fish. We didn't often kill a fish, but somehow this one fish harvested and consumed here in the canyon seemed more like a sacrament than just another meal.

The rain came gently at first. We took turns with the lantern, rustling shelters. Steve and Pat pooled their efforts, and with two oars and a tarp they constructed a tight, impromptu lean-to. Braun had his tent pitched. I strung up a small green tarp. Hard rain poured down before long and woke me in the black hours. I warmed the occasional drips with body heat and drifted back to sleep listening to the pitter of rain against the strung tarp.

The rain let up at dawn. Mist hung in the canyon. It was getting more difficult to get up early, but this was it, our last day in the canyon. Braun decided to come over with me and fish the other shore. We de-boned the shelter for oars and dragged the raft upstream to get a good angle on crossing.

Just above the first of several rapids we would float that afternoon was a fine stretch of fly water. There was a large rock at the very end that the fish liked to hold around. I told Braun the story of the Nevada dentist we had down one time when I was guiding and how he got up on top of that rock and hooked six steelhead one evening. Then I sketched the rest of the run for Braun and started back up river. I hadn't gotten a hundred yards along when I heard the yell.

I busted back down the trail and through the sagebrush and shore alders to the gravel beach where Braun was standing with a deep bend in his rod. The only sign of the fish was a slight pulsing of the tip. It was holding straight out from shore.

He turned to me with a sparkle in his eyes. "It took right out from the rock."

If it decided to drop back through the heavy chute of water, his only hope would be to chase after it. We were talking about that when the fish began moving downriver. It jumped once down in the fast water, and we could see it was an exceptionally large fish; I thought it was going for sure. Braun was nearly to shore and heading down after it when I could see from the new arc his line was cutting that the fish had changed its mind.

"It's going up," I called to him.

Braun angled back into the river and came up just below it. He reeled up all the slack so he had a straight pull on the fish, then, bending at the hip, he leaned hard on the fish. The rod bent immediately toward the water and bucked furiously while the

Upended by a steelie—he's still on though.

Photo by Ken Morrish

Judo fish—a typical pug-nosed Deschutes steelhead.

Photo by Ken Morrish

Big, open water of the lower canyon.

A favorite desert denizen. Have only seen one in many years on the river.

fish shot upriver past me. Yanks of surging line spilled off the reel. Braun slipped on the wet rocks running after it, rod high, reeling like hell.

The rest of the fight ensued smoothly in the run in front of us. Steadily pressuring the fish, he was finally able to tire it and bring it to shore. And a fine fish it was—the biggest fish of the trip, a deep twelve-pound, native—*a fine shot at the buzzer!*

Turns out it had been a good day all around. Pat landed his first fish of the trip too, across the river at the Green Light Hole, and Steve hooked two more fish in front of camp in the legendary Bathtub Hole and Cabin Hole, neither of which he was able to bring to hand. We gathered in camp that morning with the eager mid-summer sun beaming into the canyon. Dragging our butts a little from early rising and rather late night reveling, we were in no rush putting things together. Instead, we sat around in lawn chairs sipping coffee or finishing off the last of the muffins and danish or enjoying a bowl of cereal flooded with cold milk.

It seemed to me that there was satisfaction emanating from everyone. We had certainly not experienced that rare, nearly mystical state that derived from encountering waves of eager, striking steelhead moving up the river. But each of us had had some decent action and, at the very least, brought one summer steelhead to hand. And catching aside, we'd had some marvelous fishing (the heart of it, really) and a fine time in the canyon to boot. The rapids that lay ahead of us that day were the perfect ending to our journey and gave us the boost we needed to break camp one last time.

First, the ledgy, narrow, winding corridor that is Gordon's Ridge comes along not far below camp; the boats buck and spin in heavy hydraulics. A mile below, we pass between a gauntlet of fishermen in the popular Wagenblast area. Not far off my right oar a spoon gouges neatly into the green water; I don't know if it is a message or not. Ahead, the river narrows and pitches through the large standing waves of Colorado Rapid. Pat and Steve take a wall of water cleanly over their heads that rips off Pat's sunglasses and swipes both their hats. *Yow!* A couple of miles further down we approach the head of Rattlesnake.

There have been several drownings at Rattlesnake Rapid. It is rated a Class 4 (very dangerous) because of two things. The first is a giant suckhole lurking at the bottom of this fifty-yard-long rapid. At the bottom, the shore necks in on both sides and a narrow channel develops on river left, which would be easy enough to reach if it weren't for the second thing—the rocks. As you float down toward the suckhole, the river accelerates through a field of boulders. You must negotiate these, while at the same time rowing hard to get over to the left bank and away from the hole at the bottom. Worst case scenario has you messing with the boulders, getting out of control and drifting into trouble. In the words of the guidebook: "…the entire force of the Deschutes is concentrated in this suckhole." It is not the kind of place you want to stumble through.

Braun and I are the lead boat this morning. As we approach the top of the run, I pull hard on my right oar and pop it out of its oarlock! The boat drifts up on top of a rock, swings us around backward and comes to a dead stop. Water piles furiously against the upriver side of the boat as I try to remain calm and yet quickly get the oar back into the lock where it belongs. I manage this, then pull my oars hard against the powerful current. Nothing. I get up and Braun gets up and we scooch forward, but no luck. Upriver, Steve is bearing down on us and could maneuver by, but reacting quickly he cocks his boat at a twenty-degree angle, so he doesn't hang up too, and slams into our raft. It's not pretty, but it works. Drifting free, I quickly bring us under control, happily dodge a couple more boulders, and end up zipping along the left gravel bank right where we should be. Steve follows just behind, and we shoot Rattlesnake Channel safely, whooping and yelling, and we all crack a beer and toast our safe passage.

Rain returns in earnest as we push through the remaining mile or so of river. We run a final standing wave in Moody Rapid and push our boats through the frog water of enormous Moody Pool. At the take-out, a stone's throw from the broad Columbia, an androgynous-looking woman in a great yellow raincoat winches a fish onto an island in the middle of Moody Pool. Before we make it to the ramp, someone hooks another. It appears that the rain is bringing in the fish. We count ten fish hooked in the hour it takes to pack up our stuff. Granted, not all are on flies, but for barometric purposes, spoons tell the story—fish are definitely moving in. We toss around the idea of pitching our tents and staying over an extra night, hiking back upriver to fish that evening and the next morning, but the currents of obligation and circumstance at home prove stronger than the river's. We say our last good-byes to the Deschutes and get into the I-84 groove.

On the bridge over the Columbia, crossing back into Washington, we are met with a deluge. So much rain I have trouble keeping Pat's Bronco with our trailer in back from planing and I slow nearly to a crawl until it is over. It is a monotonous run up I-5. After a while I have to slap my face to ward off sleep, but Pat, rising from the ashes in the back of the truck, has a story—a long, world-caliber road story about tunneling to freedom under a Mazatlan prison in the sixties—a story that, frankly, is the most outrageous I have ever heard! It effects me like Benzedrine and takes us neatly through the sprawl of Tacoma towards the Seattle skyline, looming like Oz in the distance.

Steve Braun died early last year in a tragic kayak mishap in the San Juan Islands, where he lived. Steve was extremely active, both in his own life and within the community. Recently, he served as the president of The San Juan Preservation Trust. To celebrate his 49th birthday, two weeks before the accident, Steve made headlines in the local paper by swimming several miles to an outlying island and back. He is sorely missed.

Deschutes

The world-record fly-caught steelhead once came from the
Deschutes, a 26-pound fish caught near the mouth back in 1946 by
the Governor of Nevada. Plenty of 20-pound-plus fish swim into
the river still, although most of these fish are destined for Idaho
waters. August marks the beginning of the summer run; September
and October are peak months.

The average Deschutes steelhead is in the six to eight-pound
range. Although the ratio changes from year to year, roughly half
of the fish are hatchery progeny; the other half are native stock.

Most fishermen use a floating line, a #7 to #8 weight rod and a
well made reel with a hundred yards of backing. Standard
steelhead flies work well. Patterns tied in size #4 to #1/0 with
purple, orange, black and green as principal colors are popular.

State fishing reg's will give you the full story on what is
allowed on the river. All wild fish must be released unharmed and
all fishing is done with single barbless hooks. While the river is
open to lure fishing as well, fly fisherman are predominant.

You do have to wade the river to fish. The river has strong,
cold currents year round and most fishermen wear neoprene,
particularly first thing in the morning and last thing at dusk—
prime fly fishing times. Studs of some kind are optional, but felt
soles and a staff are a must.

Floating the river is the ultimate way to experience the
Deschutes. A guided trip down the first time is a good idea, but
with a little research, preparedness, good sense and courage,
you'll probably manage okay. Definitely though, take along the
river guidebook mentioned below and scout everything you are not
rock sure of. The best and easiest place to outfit yourself with fully
equipped boats and ice (two of the primaries), is to talk with
Donna at Deschutes U-boats. You'll run right into it on the east
side of the bridge.

Packing into the canyon on mountain bike or foot are options.
Car camping along the access roads bordering a good 20-
something miles of river around Maupin is a decent alternative as
well, but if you get on or off the river late and don't feel like
driving home, you can stay at either the Deschutes Motel or the C
& J Lodge.

While the motel is a clean and basic, fifties-vintage night on the hill above town, the lodge is a veritble oasis, situated beside the city park with a big grass lawn and shade trees running down to the water. We based a five-day trip with Judy (the J in C&J) last year when the river was in spate, and drove up river each day to fresh water, and, as it turned out, excellent trout fishing, then returned to the lodge at night. Both the food and the new glass-walled dining room are superb and Judy is a gracious host who takes pride in what she does. Personally, I liked waking up on the patio with sliced melon, pine nut pancakes and coffee and the sound of the river running while just outside the grounds a 100 degree day was underway.

Fires (or smoking outside of buildings, closed vehicles or boats) are not permitted along the river during the summer months, from June 1st through October 15th. Range fires have been a serious problem in the canyon. White gas and propane are usually permitted, although regulations can change suddenly during the peak of the season. In season, fires must be contained in a firepan. A nifty, self-contained unit called The Firepan (info below), is perfect for both cooking and a little warm up at either end of the day (by the time it's legal, you'll want it).

River water is not potable. Bring plenty.

Boaters' passes are required to float the river (obtainable in Maupin or any outlying towns all the way to Portland). Jet boats are regulated on the lower river. For a current schedule, give the BLM a call (number below).

Pick up a copy of Quinn, Quinn and King's Handbook to the Deschutes River Canyon. *You can find it in most bookstores in Oregon or you can order it directly from Educational Adventures, Inc., P.O. Box 826, Waldport, OR 97394.*

Resources:

Raft Rentals and Shuttle Info (also ice, drinks, boaters' passes and about everything else you might need):
Deschutes U-Boats
P.O. Box 144 (at east end of bridge)
Maupin, Oregon 97037
(541) 395-2503   *Continued on next page*

Lodging:
Carrol and Judy White
C&J Lodge
304 Bakeoven Road
P.O. Box 130
Maupin, Oregon 97037
800-395-3903
www.deschutesriver.com

**Guiding, Tackle and Gear
and Fishing Licenses**
Deschutes Canyon Fly Shop
John Smeraglio, proprietor
P.O. Box 334
Maupin, Oregon 97037
(541) 395-2565

The Firepan
Cambridge Welding
P.O. Box 272
Cambridge, Idaho 83610
208-257-3589

General Info:
Bureau of Land Management
Prineville District Office
185 East 4th Street
P.O. Box 550
Prineville, OR 97754
(503) 447-4115

Cocktails, Mountain Tops and the Goddess of Illusion

Photo by Author on Fuji film

'Desolation's way up there, Ray, six thousand feet or so looking into Canada . . . thousands of miles of mountains, deer, bear, conies, hawks, trout, chipmunks. It'll be great for you, Ray.'

Jack Kerouac - *Dharma Bums*

The cause of suffering is attachment.

- da Buddha

Boy, are we in a pickle. - Mickey Mouse

There is one other car at the boat-ramp parking lot at Colonial Creek when we arrive. A sixteen-foot Grumman canoe, loaded high in the middle and sunk to within inches of the gunwales, is tied to the dock. Two men, fortiesh maybe, one of them corpulent and bland, the other small and weasely looking, are preparing to push off. The big fellow is casting off the bow line while his buddy sits in the stern with a paddle in one hand, a cocktail glass in the other.

"Where you guys headin'?" I call out.

"Ross," the man on the dock answers, with a grin, while the little dude in the stern raises his glass and trills: "Cocktail anyone?"

Steve Thomsen and I look at each other a moment and think: *Where'd these clowns come from?* In the end, we look like a three-hump camel ourselves, only our boat is bigger—a homemade, 20-foot, cedar-strip design with adequate freeboard and beam. We pack it up and trim it out, joking frequently about the guys ahead of us, dubbing them Laurel and Hardy, but me thinking *darker maybe more like Lenny and George.* Finally, though, we are afloat and motor out across Diablo Lake into a deep, shadowed cleft in the mountains.

Riding on the wooden bed of the shuttle truck, our canoe bounces unmercifully. I take out a pad and slip it under the hull. We share the flatbed with the two canoeists we'd met earlier making the 600-vertical-foot portage from lower Diablo up into Ross. Curious about the fishing I lean out over the rail and shout through the driver's window.

"How's the fishing?" I say.

"Lately it's been good" he shouts back.

"It's getting late in the season, the bugs still hatchin'?"

"Chironomidae, I think, I don't do much fly fishing though, Tom's the guy to ask."

The old truck climbs steeply over a rough, reddish-rock road bed, under vine-maple cliffs, through Stygian tunnels. We hang on tight, happy to be heading into the mountains. The air is crisp, redolent with the spicy scent of pine, cooling early on an October evening. Cones litter the grade. Lights along the turbine houses below the dam gleam brightly in the fading light, then dimly as the old Chevy flatbed growls up through the gears.

The hull of our canoe is a handsome mosaic of rich browns and dark reds. Steve built it over the winter. The boat does triple duty for us; with its centerboard and square stern, it can be effectively sailed, motored or paddled. Ross Reservoir snakes its way north from Highway 20 just east of Diablo some 22 miles into the British Columbia wilderness. We would canoe up the lake in the old Skagit River Valley between the Pasayten Wilderness and the rugged Pickett Range. We were hoping to find the plentiful Ross Lake rainbows interested in our flies, spend a week in the autumn mountain air and, if the weather held, to climb Desolation Peak and bivvy a night by the legendary tower at the top.

Jack Kerouac spent a summer in the fire lookout tower cabled to the tip of Desolation and wrote of the experience in *Dharma Bums*. Gary Snyder and Allen Ginsberg were Kerouac's buddies, loosely disguised in some of his stories as Japhy Ryder and Alvah Goldbook. Kerouac had a wailing, "cut-the-shit" style and a storyline swinging wildly from coast to coast that was largely autobiographical as well. Jack's work echoed the quickening *Zeitgeist* that reigned like a minor dragon in the bourgeois mid-century air.

Kerouac's life unfolded between New York, Mexico City, and his haunts in California, but there was a period of time in the fifties when he pilgrimaged to Washington State, hitchhiking north from Marin County where he and Snyder had hiked the Muir Trail and along the flanks of Mount Tamalpais. It was Snyder's

Base of Ross Dam from the first tunnel.

Me with "Lenny," heading into Ross on
Tom's old flatbed Chevy.

Photo by Steve Thomsen

A fat Ross rainbow.

Photo by Author on Fujifilm

*Ross Lake, looking north towards Hozomeen Peak in
distant British Columbia.*

reverence for mountains that infected Jack and eventually delivered him north to the remote and soul-rending Desolation Peak. Heading to his new post on Desolation, Jack wrote: *Finally came the gray rainy day of my departure to Desolation Peak. The assistant ranger was with us, the three of us were going up and it wasn't going to be a pleasant day's horseback riding in all that downpour. "Boy, you shoulda put a couple quarts of brandy in your grocery list, you're gonna need it up there in the cold," said Happy, looking at me with his big red nose. We were standing by the corral. Happy was giving the animals bags of feed and tying it around their necks and they were chomping away unmindful of the rain. We came plowing to the log gate and bumped through and went around under the immense shrouds of Sourdough and Ruby mountains. The waves were crashing up and spraying back at us. We went inside to the pilot's cabin and he had a pot of coffee ready. Firs on steep banks you could barely see on the lake shore were like ranged ghosts in the mist. It was the real Northwest grim and bitter misery.*

We wish the cocktailing canoeists luck and head out across the lake. The little three-horse Evinrude pushes us along at six knots toward the string of floating cabins in the distance. The surface of the lake is glass, the sky devoid of clouds. No "Northwest grim and bitter misery" for us that night. Trout are dimpling everywhere!

Gobs of tiny pupal shucks litter the dark water where the insects have emerged, but we have our rods buried under all the gear and will have to wait till morning to fish. By the time we finish poking around with handkerchiefs, though, using them as seine nets to i.d. the shucks as *Chironomidae*, the hatch is over and the yellow lights from the floating camp beckon warmly across the water. It is the middle of the week, the middle of

October, and Tom Barnett has offered us a cabin for our first night on the lake.

A small fire crackles in the wood stove after dinner while Steve and I take turns huddling over a hemostat taped to the corner of the kitchen table, tying great guinea soft-hackles, and drinking Tecate in neat red cans. I drift outside frequently to languish in the cool night air, until very late when it begins to rain. Along the far shore a plume of water cascades into the lake. It rains hard that night and I wake up to the sound of it tinkling into cans in the recycling bins under my window and go outside and fix it naked. I take a moment and glance up lake in the dark, wondering how the two guys are doing.

We are up early next morning under a blue-boy sky, making espresso and pancakes on a wood stove and feeling like a million bucks. I'm cleaning the frying pan behind the cabin when I look straight down into 20 feet of water. There are trout—big trout—swarming over the bottom like snakes! One of them even comes up, snatches a bit of my cake, and splashes me with his tail.

Okay, I think, and shout to Steve who comes out to have a look. We are both down on all fours with our noses in the water.

"So that's what the sign is for," he says.

"What sign?"

"The one in the kitchen about fishing off these floats—not allowed."

"Jee-*zus,* look at the size of these guys!" It reminds me of a 'pay to fish' pond.

"This bodes good, though," he says, and I shake my head.

Walking the floating platform between the little cabins, we head to the office (stopping frequently to ogle the trout) to visit with Tom before heading out. On the wall of the office are pictures of huge Dolly Varden, rainbows, cutthroats, and piles of smiling guests. Tom gives us a tour of his floating woodshop where he spends the winter months making furniture and repairing things for the cabins. A basketball hoop is nailed to the wall of the woodshop, and we take a few minutes to shoot around in the tepid autumn sunlight.

Steve asks about Desolation.

"A party went in a week ago," Tom tells us, "but I had to rescue them on the top in a blizzard. Most of the peaks are covered with snow already. You should be okay though," he says. "There's a high pressure building in."

I have the topo out as we round Green Point in bright sun. The lake is the shape of Italy; we are starting up the boot. Over my shoulder Ruby Mountain sports a glacier on its northern flank. Due north the mountains range into the emptiness of British Columbia. I am reminded of the lake in *A Farewell to Arms,* where Catherine and the lieutenant row all night to the safety of the Swiss border. Steve throttles the engine down to an idle and we drag a couple of soft hackles out either side of the boat and relax. It is hard to relax, though, when you're constantly muttering expletives about the view.

We pass one other boat by mid-day, a couple of fishermen, and have seen no sign of anyone camping along the lake. We are curious where the other canoe might have ended up, and it is high noon when we catch sight of a plume of smoke rising from the top of Cougar Island.

As we get closer, we spot the boat.

We decide to stop and check on these guys. We pull our boat up on shore and hike the trail to the top of the little island where we find their squalid camp. The scrawny guy who brandished the cocktail the day before is more ignoble looking this morning (morning hell, it's afternoon). Wrapped in a dirty blanket and huddled around a miserable smoky fire, he is shaking with d.t.'s.

Apparently his friend is still inside the tent that has collapsed from the rain; *some*one's bare feet are sticking out. We exchange pleasantries and ask if they need anything, but don't stay long. I feel sure they don't want to chat with us any more than we do with them. It is a relief to get back under a towering blue sky and away from gloomy human degradation.

The lake is down 15 feet and even with binoculars I cannot pinpoint the camps in heavy timber, only an occasional pontoon dock resting high and dry on a steep mud embankment. We find no one pulled into half a dozen of these sites that are scattered down the lake past Cougar. The only signs of civilization now are the beached pontoons and the extraordinary suspension bridges, like miniature Golden Gates, spanning the deeper creek mouths along the west bank trail. Off Roland Point we pick up our first fish, a handsome hello rainbow flashing silver and green in the autumn air as it jumps, then darts under and all around the boat as we try and land it.

Within an hour we have two trout on ice in the Igloo. We motor toward little Cat Island, where there is still a floating dock, and get out to scope the camps. The sites are clean and well laid out, but we decide to push further down the lake in case the wind comes up and pins us down.

Near the Canadian border late that afternoon I notice a speck of something bulking small against the skyline at the tip of Desolation. I point it out to Steve: "Check that out with the binoculars; I think it's the tower."

He trains the glasses, studying a moment. "That's it all right."

We'd designated Desolation as our third-night camp on the back-country permit but, with the recent stormy weather, we had decided to play it by ear as the trip unfolded. It looked simple enough on the topo at home (only four or five miles), but from the lake you are impressed with the amount of vertical gain involved. It has no snow now at least, like Hozomeen or Ruby.

"Let's do it," Steve says quietly, smiling. Of the two of us, he is the climber. I've heard him muttering about impossible-looking Hozomeen in desirous tones. I can kick myself for not having done more to get in shape than hitchhike around the island at home for the last week, but I'm game. I hang my hand over the side and drag it in the icy water as we go along and study the route up Desolation.

We troll past Arctic Falls and up toward Little Beaver Creek and around the point along the Canadian border. We have no luck, though, and pull ashore on a point of land along the east bank at the base of Desolation and pitch camp.

Fishing the evening hatch along Boundary Bay just north of camp, we release several big trout on tiny emerger patterns. The *Chironomidae* seem to fill the lake. We take turns casting from the bow, great yanks of fish grabbing our tiny flies on every cast and teasing high-pitched shrieks from our reels until suddenly like a switch at dark the fish turn off and we paddle the short distance to camp.

A little breeze comes up around our fire that night. In lantern and campfire light, the exposed clay lake bed and tree stump forest around camp is eerie looking. When I go off to pee, the shadows are bizarre. When the government dammed the Skagit, the loggers cut down the trees but did not stump the shore in advance of the rising waters. In icy water the stumps remain well preserved. The ones along shore, at least, will eventually decompose, as they are exposed to air for much of the season. Still tizzed from the excellent fishing that evening, we nip from a bottle of Canadian whiskey while we roast fried trout, onions, and potatoes on a two-burner Coleman. Across the lake we can hear the incessant, dull roar of Arctic Falls waxing louder at odd moments with the wind. The call of loons drifts over the lake and the occasional old Skagit River rock exploding in the fire punctuates the first half of the final chapter of *Dharma Bums* that I read aloud after we've eaten and cleaned up and have our pipes lit around the fire.

We spend the better part of the next day climbing Desolation, aiming for timberline and respite from ravaging mosquitoes. The trail is an unrelenting five-thousand-foot gain in altitude. Vagrant shafts of light penetrate the canopy and light up the brilliant reds and yellows of the understory.

The trail passes tree line when we gain Starvation Ridge, then forks. We are pouring sweat as we make the juncture, but the mosquitoes are thinning at least. A bite of lunch there in the meadow, then we metabolize the bagel and cheese into steam along the ridgeline running north until, finally, we come upon a lonely looking tower perched like a witch's cabin on the summit of Desolation Peak. The view of Hozomeen, behind, accentuates the eeriness.

We stop for a minute at dusk to grovel for tiny huckleberries in the dense shrubbery before huffing the last 200 yards, but spend more energy picking than we get in return. I notice there is bear shit all along the trail at this altitude. The gnarled and twisted trees at 6000 feet resemble stone trolls. Approaching the cabin, we hear a mysterious cooing sound coming from the wooden structure; something runs out from beneath . . . a pair of blue grouse.

It is dark early and we sit up huddled in our down bags with our backs against the tower blocks, listening to the whistling wind and the nesting grouse, who sound in love, to me. We have surveyed the tower and found the window covered with Visquene and tape where the rescued party broke in to ride out the storm but cannot in good conscience break in ourselves. Instead we huddle around our tiny gas stove, which we guess can be seen from every other mountain top within a 100 miles, then, laughing, guess how many inhabited mountain tops that just might be. It is a fine clear night.

We drink blackberry tea and cognac and finish the last of *Bums*. I put away the book and turn out the flashlight. There are stars everywhere and sparks from our pipes. We refill our cups and discuss the meaning of "Dharma" and try to define "bum."

We decide that between a wise man and a fool lies a curious line, thin as a wisp of steam one moment, impenetrable as steel the next. The Dharma bum was the wise man searching out his essence—the karma bum, the fool.

"To bums," Steve toasts.

"To all bums . . . everywhere," I add, feeling the blessing of my own evolving bumdom from sex-bum to psychedelic-bum to river-and fly-fishing-bum, on to writer and adventure-bum (never losing any of the stages altogether, though). Never a straight-away Dharma bum, for sure, but rather always pursuing the things that burned most fiercely in my soul. Spinning a bit from the cognac, altitude, and heady thoughts, I lie down and try to sleep but when I see the Challenger shuttle pass overhead going lickety-split I sit up straight and shout to Steve . . . then it's gone. After I tuck myself in again and begin to nod off, the wind picks up. Fast and hard. Within minutes it is pushing through my zipper baffle and breaking into the tower is looking more conscionable by the moment.

It's a bitch getting in. I squeeze through the window headfirst and somersault to the floor. Steve passes our packs through. It is like night and day being out of the demon wind, though, and we explore around with our flashlights. Heavy plywood shutters are fastened down over the windows and the walls are painted an institutional green. A theodolite hunkers in the center of the room; Steve shows me how it works. There is a desk and a propane stove, a sink, some tools and survival gear, and plenty of back-up stuff. We find a drawer full of journals and pour through them. I am disappointed to find that none go further back than five years . . . I was half hoping to find one of Jack's.

It is a little strange being in the cabin as we are, technically illegal and with the windows boarded up and the wind hammering and frosty cold, too, but we dig it. The high mountain storm whistles under the rafters as the little building shudders against the strongest blasts, and we take comfort knowing the hut is anchored to the mountain with cables as thick as our arms. We aren't ready to sleep and it seems like a fine idea anyway so we decide to brew up a pot of tea. Not blackberry this time either, but hemp.

"Kerouac died an alcoholic," Steve argues later.

"So what?" I say. "So did Watts and Hemingway. Their lives weren't the inspiration, for the most part . . . their work was."

"What about Snyder in this? He's more the role model, if anyone is."

I think about this a minute. "For sure, it was Snyder that really walked the talk, went to Japan to live the Buddhist life, lived like a monk, still does . . . still, Jack's characters were the only hipsters most of us will ever know and his better work is an awesome synthesis of poetry and prose."

The water is nearly to a boil, the MSR stove roaring louder than the wind. I find a passage set on the peak and read it aloud nearly shouting: *Lo, in the morning I woke up and it was beautiful blue sunshine sky and I went out in my alpine yard and there it was, everything Japhy said it was, hundreds of miles of pure snow-covered rocks and virgin lakes and high timber, and below,*

Photo by Author on Fujifilm

Looking east over Ross into the Pasayten Wilderness.

Photo by Steve Thomsen

Our camp at the base of Desolation.

Working a long line during a chironomidae hatch.

Another nice Ross bow.

instead of the world, I saw a sea of marshmallow clouds flat as a roof and extending miles and miles in every direction, creaming all the valleys, on my 6600-foot pinnacle it was all far below me. I brewed coffee on the stove and came out and warmed my mist-drenched bones in the hot sun of my little woodsteps. I said "Tee tee" to a big furry cony and he calmly enjoyed a minute with me gazing at the sea of clouds.

It is a strange, sweet, mystical night. The tea is warm against the hands, hot to the lips, and only slightly bitter in the frosty air of our cell. The only sadness is that we cannot see out from the tower with the shutters bolted down. With the tea, finally, comes the magic. It is a good, penetrating high and I poke around the tower leisurely in the moment, stopping every now and then where I can feel the air seeping in around a window and push my nose into the crack . . . *aaah!* Our breath frosts in the chill air, but I am dressed in gloves and pile and down and feeling a little numb to temperature anyway.

I do not want to talk; I am well beyond my mouth. Steve is brushing his teeth and going to bed. Ganja puts him down.

Thoroughly stoned, I end up on my cot, slip in a pair of ear-plugs, put out the lights and groove in the dark a while. Sinking well below the conceptual stage, I flow with the story line each thought elicits. I sit up straight, cross-legged, meditating and remain so for hours. I recall . . . *Berkeley, sitting in meditation on a corner of the campus at midnight peaking on acid when to my most profound amazement my mind drops into stillness, the wheel of thoughts like a slot machine—slowing from thought to thought. . . to. . . thought. . . suddenly to a complete stop, my mind transformed into utter calm and oneness with universal Mind. . . .* Not on my agenda tonight, though: it is a wandering meditation, and I am not able to stay with my mantra but go off on a chain of colored journeys, drawn back time and again to a blast of wind.

Late into the night with the return of lucidity I am visited, like Ebeneezer's ghost of Christmases past, by my own nemesis.

In my stoneness I realize my predilection for Kerouac over Snyder; a basic, irrefutable thing. It is affinity, for I too am more like the weaker, alcoholic Kerouac than I am like Snyder. I am not the *bhikku*, the pure spiritual seeker. I am the hobbled, the habituated, the attached. Only by conscious choice do we climb from Plato's cave; I know this abstractly, yet remain transfixed by the timeworn shadows. I toy at the truth, long ago adopting meditation as discipline, as spiritual insurance, while I feed ambition and sensual nature. An erection in one hand—stick of incense in the other.

From sex bum to river bum, the works . . . all issues from between the legs of Maya, Goddess of illusion. It is certainly in the female of the species that I find the most potent alchemy. I remember one *Mahayana* passage stating that it is in the form of woman that Maya is most at home. *No wonder I'm preoccupied with sex; when I'm lying with Pamela, I'm lying with a Goddess.*

Nose to the womb, nose to the wheel. I am seeing all this pretty clearly tonight and feeling a tempered form of angst to the tragedy of not transcending it. Tempered, because it is not the first such visit; tempered, because it is intrinsic to the human condition. I figure truth is like a dog waiting patiently at the door to go out and pee; sooner or later I'll notice it. Mercifully, sleep overtakes such rumination in the wee morning hours.

We sit on the steps of the cabin in the sun, drinking coffee, waking up, coming around. It is not early. The intense self-awareness of the night before, at least, has evaporated with the coffee and fresh air like the dew steaming off the tower walls behind us. I get up and go over to the window to secure the tape and plastic as best I can and it seems symbolic, the window does.

Handy all right to get in out of a storm—handy to transcend our everyday perspective for a quick look around. *There is no great future in windows though,* I'm thinking, *yet I'm surely not ready for the door.*

A paste of white fog covers the lake below. "They have parafoils now," Steve tells me, "that you can pack up a mountain. Only thirty pounds or so."

I am stiff and sore from yesterday's grunt and could use a parafoil. We would be braking going down, at least, and using a different set of muscles.

We stalk around our alpine domain a while, sipping coffee, putting our packs together, and making small discoveries around the tower. Nothing is witchy in the morning light. The tower has a single lightening rod on its pyramid roof and four heavy copper wires running down the corners of the cabin to ground. At each of the four corners concrete blocks are pinioned into bedrock. The cables that we trusted in last night are firmly guyed out. The cabin isn't going anywhere.

We continue north that afternoon, our legs thrown up over the gunwale and our aching backs pushed deeply into cushioned backrests. The descent of Desolation had been uneventful—five hours up, less than half that coming down.

Motoring the lake is samadhic. The purr of the little gas motor vibrates through the hull. I can feel it in my lowest chakra and begin to get aroused. I remember last night and think, *jeez what an idiot . . .* then I laugh suddenly, feeling just fine about it. We pass Little Jackass Mountain and the ranger station at Hozomeen and are well into British Columbia for lunch. Then it is my turn to sit in the sunny stern by the cooler, doling out pop or beer and using the clever steering arm Steve has rigged up. I fire up the little motor, then idle it way down. I pick up my rod and unhook a handsome chartreuse soft hackle from the hook-keeper and slowly let out line.

We motor back down the lake that afternoon, heading for Barnett's floating cabins for a night of decompression before heading out. We catch our dinner again, several fine, green-backed, fighting trout. They nail our flies with a vengeance. Within sight of the dam, we notice a boat closing quickly behind us.

A Boston Whaler heads for us like a shot; it looks like the ranger.

I shut down our kicker as he comes about.

"You fellows seen another canoe today?" he calls over.

Steve and I look at each other and shake our heads.

"I found some gear. . . paddles, sleeping bags and life jackets floating near Cougar Island," he says. "When I saw your boat, I thought it might be a couple of other guys I'd written a back-country permit for earlier this week. Seen anything at all?"

The fate of the two canoeists is still a mystery to us. The shuttle driver reported not having shuttled them back down to Diablo. To my knowledge no bodies have ever been found. My guess is they swamped their boat and swam ashore, then hiked up to high-way 20 and were gone. Cocktailin' is a whole lot easier in the city.

For more info on the floating resort at Ross, call Tom @ (206) 386-4437.

Middle Fork Journal

Photo by Author on Fujifilm

. . .Time is like a flowing river—
One day we wake up old men . . .

Han Shan, untitled poem

Water is to God, as rivers are to man.

Anonymous

Appeared originally in *Outside - On-line*

An early dusting of snow covered the ragged Sawtooth Range; with my forehead pressed against the cold glass, I watched the shadow of our little plane track across it. My wife Pamela and I, her daughter Mia, and Mia's husband Ken Morrish, were four of a party of 12 fishermen flying into the heart of the vast Idaho Primitive Area. Barren ridge lines dusted with snow cut steeply into deep, rocky, sparsely timbered canyons, one after another as far as the eye could see. Streams thinly lined the canyons. Water was typically sparse the first week in September in the mountains of Southern Idaho. The fall of '97 was especially so, and extremely low water had forced our guides to float the boats down from a launch point along the upper river two days prior to our arrival. Without the extra weight of the clientele and baggage, they hoped to have an easier time of it; even then, we found out, it was rough going nicking boats on rocks and beaching them on gravel bars.

Ken and I had wanted to float the Middle Fork for a long time, not just for the wilderness and the white water, but to sample its much-touted fishery. Mia was anticipating fishing too. With a degree in Environmental Ed, she was at home in the outdoors from New Zealand to Alaska. Pamela was a fisherwoman as well, although purely a pragmatic one. Although she had caught trout, bass, bluegill, even steelhead on a fly before, Pamela was a down-to-earth *catch and eat* kind of girl. No toying with life forms for her, thank you. Pamela's idea of adventure was paddling the open ocean off the coast of British Colombia; her interest in the Middle Fork was quite simply to experience it.

Although I'd heard about the river since I was a kid, I knew little more about it, really, than that it was the longest free-flowing river in the continental States and that it was remote, rambunctious, and stuffed with trout—easily enough adjectives to put it on *my* calendar. So, when Kitty Shelton, owner of Middle

Fork Wilderness Outfitters, invited the four of us out on a late fall trout fishing trip, their last trip of the season, we jumped at the chance.

The air was crisp under diamond stars when we left the elegant Idaho Country Inn, in Ketchum, early that same morning in September. We piled into a company school bus, drinking coffee and munching croissants, as we motored north into the mountains of Southern Idaho. We arrived finally at Stanley, a log-cabin and Quonset-hut town set deep in the Idaho back country, and jump-off point for the interior.

The weather was sour looking, cool and windy, and a summer's worth of dust whirled like dervishes through the quiet streets. Pat Deal was our liaison. Dressed in shorts, hiking boots, and sunglasses, his ski patrol cagoule flapping against his bare legs and a wad of chew bulging his lower lip, he cut a dashing figure. Like many river guides, Pat worked the winter season with the ski patrol in the popular resorts of the Rockies and Sierra mountains. After ducking into the office of McCall Air, he emerged, frowning, having confirmed what he had expected. Planes were grounded in McCall; good news, though, was they expected a break in the weather sometime that afternoon.

Just after midday there was, indeed, a respite from scudding, gray clouds. By this time most of us had burrowed into our piles of luggage heaped on the wind-swept tarmac of the airfield. Soon, we heard the drone of planes in the distance, and, finally we caught sight of three tiny, flyspeck aircraft coming down the valley.

"Zee plane! Zee plane," someone yelled.

Pat and the pilots got together and talked things over. Finally, Mike, the head pilot, decided to give it a go. Loaded up with a full complement of passengers and gear, he lifted off to see how conditions were just over a nearby ridge. We watched him loop around in the distance and return to the airfield.

"Little bumpy still," he told us. "Should be better before long."

Sure enough, an hour later we were aloft, bumping along on an easterly heading toward the juncture of a tributary of the Middle Fork. A little plane in turbulent air can be a frightening experience; I still haven't flown enough to get completely used to it (I've been out on a turbulent ocean in a kayak often enough, though, and been tossed around in similar fashion). Half an hour later we caught our first glimpse of the Middle Fork, descended several thousand feet into the deep "V" of a moderately forested canyon, and followed an unimpressive looking ribbon of water south.

An unseasonably dry summer had the river drooping in its banks. From the air it looked like little more than wet rock. Before long we spotted our other plane sitting on a tiny air strip; pulled up on a nearby beach were what looked to be a small fleet of colorful rafts. Our pilot radioed down and, after a brief conversation, we banked hard left into a shallow side canyon.

Dicey place to hang a U, I thought.

It looked to me as if there were no room to make the turn. To make matters worse, the stall alarm went off, making an ominous, death-knell sound. I looked quickly at Pamela, and she looked as wide-eyed as I'm sure I was. I couldn't see much of the pilot behind his earphones and sunglasses, but he didn't seem concerned, nor did he say anything to assuage our fears. A moment later I could make out a route between a rock spire and the cliff itself and we safely made it through. But then, instead of tipping our nose into a descent, we continued north up the canyon, leaving the airstrip at Indian Creek behind.

A little ways ahead we could see a bit of shelf in the canyon wall. It was quite flat and appeared to be a landing strip of some type; I had seen it on the way in and wondered what it was. It was perched several hundred feet above the river on a narrow rock shelf with no obvious trails leading anywhere. It looked like the airstrip from hell to me, something the Anasazi might have used. Our plane landed safely on the short runway, however, running clear to the end of the cliff where the pilot pivoted the plane and turned to us: "Two of you get out here. Lighten the load. Our other pilot reported water on the runway. So, for safety's sake, I'll take two of you now, and come back for the rest."

Indeed, the landing at Indian Creek was a piece of work. With the plane having run fully to the end of another very short, very wet runway, nearly touching noses with the other plane and throwing a blinding deluge of water over the windshield, I was very happy to have my feet back on solid ground. And as we watched our third and last plane land safely, I was stroking myself for having optioned for the bus shuttle at trip's end, instead of another small-plane odyssey.

A row of smiling faces lined up to greet us along the edge of the tarmac. Kitty and her husband Gary Shelton were there, along with Eric Rector, co-owner of Middle Fork Adventure Outfitters, a family-run operation with a sole focus on the Middle Fork. The flight was quickly forgotten and the charms of the river took us in hand. Beyond a small fleet of boats, including one odd- looking unit that resembled a floating corral, was the river. From the air, the river had seemed thin and pallid; standing beside it was a different story. The water was icy cold as I knelt down to touch it, and it was a looker, too; although it was largely gin clear, there were patches and sleeves of a mysterious deep green color. It ran probably half the size of the Deschutes and came bowling down the canyon like a gang of roller-skaters on a Venice Beach boardwalk.

It was a good 75 miles overall to our take out on the main stem

Photo by Ken Morrish

Mia Morrish with a rather nice fish.
Cover reproduced by permission of California Fly Fisher.

Salmon four days hence. Because of our delays that day, we would have to hustle to make our first night's camp. Pamela and I picked the furthermost boat on the beach where Eric Lieberman, or "Lieb" as he's called, introduced himself as our guide and pushed us off. Pamela took the front seat and I got in the back where I hoped to be out of everyone's way while I wet a line. The back seat of a raft in rough water is like riding the fluke of a whale. It was a rollercoaster through the rapids, and I had to hang on to keep from getting bucked overboard. *So much for solid ground,* I thought.

Meanwhile, I fished. Lieb helped out whenever he could and swung the boat near the best-looking water. We were not in so much of a rush that we couldn't do justice to the choicest spots. I fished some fine looking boulder pockets, eddies, and undercut banks in the first few miles and got some half-hearted takes and the occasional trout, but it seemed the fish just weren't inclined to surface that afternoon. We could see trout, though, suspended in the upper water column.

We were rowing to make up time; meanwhile, I did my best to adjust to everything at once—to maintain my balance, carry on a conversation with Lieb, and keep 15 feet of line in motion all at the same time. I tied on a favorite hopper pattern, something the river's famous for, and touched it down for a quick float behind a rock here, or sent it chattering quickly through a fishy looking riffle there, or shot it out tight against a bank with a bit of over-hanging sedge. At one point I hung up on something and snapped my tip trying to free it, a stupid mistake. Thinking maybe my blood sugars were dropping, I dug out a PowerBar and gnawed on it while I cased my broken rod and carefully extracted two segments of a little #3 wt. Hexagraph.

There was little sign of insects, an occasional golden stone buzzing around, the token hopper drifting past. It was cool still,

One of the many black bear in the Middle Fork Canyon.

A resident Middle Fork Western Slope Cutthoat.

Photo by Ken Morrish

Eric Rector working some nice water.

and Lieb thought the low pressure had put the fish off. I knew I should probably tie on a nymph, but there was just so much going on that I didn't bother. I figured at least a big dry was easy to keep track of.

I noticed Lieb had been pushing the boat along through the flat stretches; that made sense. But this particular stretch of canyon held a pocketful of Class 2 and 3 rapids, and we had taken each of them like Picabo Street, Idaho's own *enfant terrible*. It was Toad's wild ride to be sure, especially from the rear of the bus. I asked Lieb about this downriver rowing business; where I came from we all back-rowed through rapids.

"The Portagee method," he called over his shoulder. "Trick is to use the momentum of the river to your advantage, become one with the flow. Instead of fighting it by back rowing," he told me, "you use the currents to your advantage."

I had to admit that if it were me in the center seat, we might still be half a mile back upriver, and I had to admire the way we had *shushed* through the rock gardens that afternoon. Although this was most definitely a preferred method for these experienced oarsmen, I found it hard to relax with.

We were close to camp when I had enough of a handle on things to bother with a nymph. Even then, a nymph dropper tied below my Stimulator was a compromise. Soon thereafter, however, I set on a pair of heavy fish in succession, landing one and losing the other. By the time we reached camp at Marsh Creek, the sun had left the canyon and the air was chilling fast. We were all looking forward to moving around and getting the blood circulating.

Reports from the other boats that afternoon were mostly similar to our own, moderate and subsurface. Ken (later voted Fisherman of the Year in the company newsletter) and Mia had done well, running a little bead-head nymph below a parachute hopper and taking a dozen fish up to 14 inches between them. Mia is no stranger to big fish; you may have seen her on the Oct. '96 cover of *California Fly Fisher,* cradling a rainbow the size of a dachshund.

The temperature plummeted quickly in the deep shadows of the canyon as we set up our tents and changed into warm clothing. It felt good to finally anchor on the firmament. At the upriver end of the flat was a small hot spring which many folk pilgrimaged to over the course of the evening. Following a cocktail or two and a briefing on safety and procedural issues, we dove into plates of hot pizza from Kitty's fleet of Dutch ovens.

Kitty Shelton is one energetic woman. Part owner of the company, she is also mother to two girls (one of whom, Holly, came along on our trip as a guide in training). She is a certified guide herself and the author of *Recipes From the Middle Fork.* With the aid of her iron ovens (cleverly stacked three or four high between beds of coals), we devoured an astounding array of pastries, pies and steaming entrees over the course of the week. Fishing aside, a person could do this trip for the food alone.

Awake quite early the next morning, we found ice in the water bottles outside our tent. There was also blue sky above a towering canyon of iron shadow. Before we got up, Pat came along with huge mugs of coffee, knocked on our tent flap, and with a big smile handed them down. The first touch of sunlight rimmed the canyon like lip gloss half a mile overhead as I made my own pilgrimage to the springs, hiking the long ponderosa flat through dewy grass and a feathering mist. Leaning against black rock, I swirled hot water around my legs and sipped my second coffee.

Ken showed up before long, looking for a shot of the springs. He decided we needed somebody with less body hair than me in the tub, though, and went looking for the women. Mia was not an option, she explained to Ken with a *don't-waste-your-breath* look on her pretty face, and he went off in search of her mother, whom he finally persuaded to pose.

We climbed aboard with Lieb again that morning, and Burt Cayson joined us. Burt had come out from Texas with two long-term fishing buddies, Bill Hayden and Howard Guess. They were great folks on something like this and set a tone of easy companionship for the group. In this age of high tech equipment, it was a relief to watch someone like Burt. Using his favorite old South Bend fiberglass fly rod and automatic fly reel, the man flat-out caught fish. With a quiet *jodevrie,* Burt went about fishing, nothing rushed, or deliberated about it, he just sat at ease, catching fish, conducting a kind of trout *darshan* in the front of the boat.

Our boats were staggered half a mile along the river. Occasionally we would leapfrog each other if one of the boats was fishing a back eddy or pulled ashore for something. We saw very few other boats or outfitters along the river. Drifting alternately in and out of deep shadow and bright sunlight, the effect was like an accordion on our susceptible bodies—swooning into warmth with a deep sigh one moment, sporting goose pimples the next.

With the near constancy of a midday sun, we began to relax. The fragrance of sagebrush and pine and mineral-rich river water were enhanced in the warming air. In exquisite sunlight, the river became a bouquet of intensely white blooms and black-hole greens so dark they sucked on the eyes. With the sun, the hoppers limbered up their stiff knees, and the hunt was afoot. Flushed with a mix of color, nitrogen, roaring coolness, the sweep and rock of the little boat, and then the frying rays of the sun, I took off my pile coat, then my shirt and began fishing with a relish.

In the immensity of this primitive area, wildlife flourishes. Mule deer, black bear, mountain goat, and bighorn sheep are common. Rocky Mountain elk thrive here as well. Golden eagles and red-tailed hawks soar high up in the canyon corridor. Kingfishers complain loudly when humanfishers enter their territory. A family of river otter appeared from time to time, as playful as a passel of kids. In the side canyons, we heard the call of the chukar or maybe a drumming grouse.

We negotiated a rapid, and the river swung left, roiling over a field of sunken boulders. Along the shore, sprigs of sedge raked the surface. In the lee of one hummock, I could see into the river as through thick, green glass; four black, oblong shapes finned just under the surface like miniature U-boats.

Quickly, I delivered my hopper and checked my cast. The fly dropped lightly to the surface and I skittered it across the pool. The boat was absolutely sailing by as I lurched over the pontoon, extended my arm to its limit, trying to leave the little mouthful in the little pool just as long as I possibly could. Then *yes!*—a black shape materialized, levered open a quick white mouth and shot up into the air!

Lieb pulled magnificently on his oars and gave me precious seconds, but it was anticlimactic. I leaned very hard on this fish, six pounds or so of pressure onto four-pound tippet, but fate pressed inexorably. The rod bent deeply, the line thrummed audibly as the trout surged upstream against the current and a shrieking reel.

Then it was over, my long line dragging in the river. "Okay," I said to Lieb, with nothing in my voice, and he glanced over his shoulder and lifted his oars.

Later that day in Jackass Rapid we lost Tom Dixon overboard. Tom had been sitting on the rear pontoon, opposite me, when the boat careened off a rock. He hung on grimly to the safety rope as the boat spun out of control through the rapid. At the bottom we slammed up against a rock ledge with Tom sandwiched between. He shrugged it off as we hauled him in, explaining that he had been cushioned by his life preserver. His wife Linda was re-lieved to have him back aboard, though, and was crying.

Again, Lieb and I discussed this Portagee technique. Sure, I could see it was a quicker, more efficient system . . . so what? It was damn tough to recover when you got off line, and the smack from rowing *into* something was not a subtle experience. We car-omed through some challenging white water that week, but to Lieb's credit Tom's dunking was our only incident.

We were in fishing heaven that day, as well as the days to come. There was plenty of good-looking water and plenty of fish, a refreshing indulgence of one-half of the fishing cycle. The fishy-looking edges with overhanging flora were best. What the cutthroat lacked in terms of challenge, casting successfully into such places provided in sheer visceral satisfaction.

You could tell these Middle Fork fish had been working out. At the quietest of times, this river moves with a sense of purpose; the hell flows of spring runoff are an annual Ironfish event. The Middle Fork trout are a buff bunch, having evolved swimming the vigorous currents of this river. And they seem a touch faster than your average trout; one moment your fly is floating beside the boat, the next it's on the bottom of the river in someone's mouth.

We were talking with Eric Rector one evening around the fire. I asked him to sum up the bug scene for us. He told us: "The salmon fly hatch, the big Pteronarcys, comes off about the sec-ond or third week in June, and runs for about two or three weeks. Following that, are the goldens, probably the most dominant bug on the river; they drag on through the summer. Then, of course, there are the hoppers. We have a strong, *really* strong, hopper hatch. We've been fishing hoppers now since mid-July. Maybe a caddis pattern or a Stimulator early or late in the day, but by and large it's hoppers, and a Parachute Hopper at that. I would have to say that, from our experience at least, the Parachute Hopper is probably 20 percent more effective on this river than any of the other hopper patterns. And the more serious fishermen might want to fish a "hopper dropper," which is a hopper on top with a small mayfly nymph or caddis larvae, or maybe a bead-head nymph, trailing on a couple-foot length of fine tippet.

Over the course of the week we found that by switching back and forth between adult stone patterns (larger stimulators and sofa pillows) and hoppers, we had equally good results. It dawned on me that with an overlapping golden emergence; any down-wing pattern, even an October caddis, would be suggestive of the general silhouette of any of the big three—*hoppers, big caddis, or stones*. I'm sure the salmon fly hatch would produce a selective period of feeding, maybe the goldens too when they came off in good numbers, but these hungry cutts in fast water were not seriously differentiating between tent-wing and flat-wing status, even, it seemed, in variation in underbody coloration. Furthermore, I found that not only had I simplified my patterning choices, but I had simplified my water interpretation as well. Although there was a respectable amount of cover and structure to fish to, by the end of the second day I noticed I was keying my casts to *color* as much as anything else.

When I first became aware of this, the idea seemed simplistic. When I thought about it further, I realized it was actually an old story. From farm pond to creek to river, it was color that had always spoken dirtiest to me. The richest greens and deep sea blues, especially, were the stuff of wanton seduction. Pragmatic too, I simply did well in such places. Colored water meant limited visibility and shelter, something fish sought out in the middle of the day to hide from predators. Anadromous fish in particular often hug the bottom of the deepest holes in the river, the deep

All photos by Ken Morrish

Views of the Middle Fork Canyon

Photo by Author on Fujifilm

The Middle Fork Wilderness Outfitters crew. Whitey, John, Holly, Lieb, Kitty, Gary, Peter, Pat and Eric. Good looking bunch!

Photo by Pamela Maresten

The author with Ken Morrish, incognito.

blue or green waving like a flag to a fisherman. Deepening color demarcated depth, shadow, or plant life, all of which are fishy issues. And this seemed to be more the case on the middle fork of the Salmon than anywhere I could remember fishing. The river that week was a palette of greens: forest, Kelly, apple, and spring green along with moss, jade, celadon and emerald.

There is elegance in the reduction of elements. My wife is a visual artist, and I have learned much from her world. A Henry Moore sculpture, a cello solo by Yo-Yo Ma … or fishing. Maybe it's the way of the maturing angler that carries him toward simplicity and away from complexity. I don't know. But I do know that less and less often do I rack my brain when I'm on the water, and more and more am I feeling the river and enjoying the colors and looking for the subtle, simple approach; fishing by color that week on the Middle Fork was essentially that.

A river of sparse strokes, the Middle Fork, rushing water over granite bottom, little flora in a narrow riparian zone bordering shore, few snags in the watercourse. A hard-bottomed, ice-cold stream without an excess of limestone or phytoplankton in suspension (Lieb does tell us, though, there are brine shrimp). Gravel bars are bleached and orderly, and little silt gathers along the bottom. There is no mud. There are occasional sand bars where the river makes its deposit each year (popular camp sites). It is a river flushed clean, flushed to bedrock each winter, a twisting flowage of shadow and cleaving light that is easy on the eyes.

Nights are clear and cold in the canyon in September. I had the distinct impression I was standing at the hub of a huge roulette wheel as the planet spun ponderously on its axis. The coming of shadow, presaging darkness, feels ominous at times (when you are wet and cold especially the river seems threatening), and the cold light of early morning little more than a premonition.

But soon rays beamed over 90 million miles flood the canyon like a warm bath, and the midday winds kick in and scour out the stubborn chill hugging the canyon floor. The hoppers wake up and shake a leg, and the fishing is afoot.

The dominant fish in the system is the indigenous Middle Fork Western Slope Cutthroat. The cutts range typically from ten to 18 inches, with rainbows averaging ten to twelve. Eric told us that the proportion of cutthroat to rainbow is a fluctuating ratio of maybe 10 or 20 to one. There are Dolly Varden, or bull trout, as well, although we didn't see any. A small run of steelhead still return to the river, well-colored after their exhausting journey, nearly a thousand miles in from the coast. The Chinook salmon, once a presence here, are fighting a difficult battle to survive. Returns to Marsh Creek, one of the first stops for salmon spawning in the state, are grim. Environmental author Rocky Barker reported that in 1964, 1400 salmon spawned in the creek, while in 1990 only 100 spawned, and in 1995 it was down to zero. Redfish Lake, headwaters of the Middle Fork and once the spawning grounds for over a million sockeye salmon, is now devoid of even one. Redfish is a top rung on the Columbia Basin endangered fish scene, and a sad testimony to a blundering society. With the trout heading the same direction early in the century, the Idaho Fish and Game stepped in to establish a "Catch and Release" fishery, with artificials only and a single barbless hook. The trout, nowadays, are doing well.

The Middle Fork was home to the Sheepeater Indians, a separate tribe of the Shoshoni Indian Nation, who lived in the canyon for thousands of years before the coming of the white man. Pamela and Mia and I hiked a six-mile stretch of trail one afternoon and found several caves with pictographs stained into the rock walls. It was easy to imagine a young hunter hunkering on the cave floor, working on a drawing while waiting out a storm. On one cave wall we found a drawing of a stick figure sporting a woody; behind him were 25 marks—quarry, no doubt, of one kind or another. In the late 1800s a few hardy miners and hermits entered the canyon. Early in the 1900s parts of the canyon were homesteaded. Nowadays, only a couple of sites remain, grandfathered into the public domain.

Surrounding the canyon, the Idaho Primitive Area yawns to nearly 2500 square miles as the largest protected wild area in the lower states. The feeling of remoteness is tangible. Not only are you sitting at the bottom of a deep fissure in the earth, but it is a long, long way out to anywhere. No motorized craft are allowed on the Middle Fork, and the Forest Service strictly limits the numbers of both commercial and private parties allowed on the river per day. Outfitters are monitored to ensure that garbage and waste are removed with each party.

The river has over 100 tributaries, 30 different rapids with a Class 3 or higher rating, and all the energy typical of the young, which these mountains are. As the river descends from its headwaters at 7000 feet, it passes through a varied, changing terrain. High in its course, it is heavily forested, mostly Doug fir. Midway down, it dries up considerably and gets little snow in winter. The airy lodgepole pine and its bigger brother, the ponderosa, lend an aura of dignity to these austere environs. Near its confluence with the main-stem Salmon, sagebrush appears as the river takes in its belt a notch to pass through towering canyon walls.

We sat down to a fresh blue tablecloth, silverware, candlelight, and wine glasses our last night in the canyon. After an excellent meal, we pulled our camp chairs around a crackling pine fire under a brilliant bank of stars: theater night with an old west flavor, the staff dressed up in bow ties and clean faces, with their ever-present sunglasses suspended *de rigueur* behind their necks from colorful Chums. While the rest of us settled into the sand with our drinks, Lieb and a couple of other guides delivered a fresh recital of the Robert Service epic, "The Cremation of Sam McGee." As I sat listening, I could feel the camaraderie among the staff. From the early days of Woody Hinton and the legendary Helfrich family of Rogue and Umpqua fame to the current generation of canyon cowboys on the challenging Middle Fork, the position of guide has been a rich and time-honored one.

I hitched a ride aboard the sweep our last morning out. Steep-walled canyons lay ahead of us with rapids, narrow chutes, and cool, moist air. An enigmatic young Australian and veteran sweep driver named Peter Spiers directed me to a corner of the boat where I would be out of his way. The boat was an enormous (perhaps 15 by 25 feet) black, Hypalon pontoon affair with canvas skirting running the perimeter. It had a removable gangplank for swampers to haul cargo in and out and plywood decking over storage compartments below. Loaded down, trimmed out, and buttoned up, it was rather like a floating cabinet laid on its back. It was easy to imagine on a river like the Mississippi, but I had to wonder how it managed on a river like the Middle Fork.

"They have a long history on the river," Peter told me, as he stood amidships, one foot forward, his shoulder facing downstream, the handle of a long ashen rudder in each hand.

Sitting atop the swiftest part of the water column, the sweeps act like rudders against the slower level. It was the Portagee method, without oars. Riding the currents was one thing, getting out into them was another. Peter actually pushed the boat broadside to the current to inch our way to center channel where we quickly drifted from sight. The sense of the thing did not jump right out at me, I confess, but when Peter let me have a hand at

Buddhist boatman, Peter Spiers.

Photo by Author on Fujifilm

the wheel it suddenly not only made sense, but oh how quickly the poetry, the physicality of the boat came across. Standing on the steering platform with the sweeps in my hands, I felt an old and strangely familiar sense of connection. I remembered how, when I ran drift boats on Oregon rivers, I had a similar feeling when I would stand at the oars and feel the sweep of the river beneath my feet. More interesting than even the sweep boat, though, was its driver.

Imagine a cross between Meriwether Lewis and a monk, or John Wesley Powell and a monk, or hell, just old Han Shan himself, and you have a Peter Spiers. Peter is a guy with a foot in the best of two worlds—a travel-loving, adventure-seeking *bhikku*. No less rugged than the older school of sportsman, a Peter Spiers of this generation might be inclined to sit a moment in meditation along the river come cocktail hour preceding a large, deadthing dinner. In the off season, Peter travels in Europe and Asia, running rivers and visiting Buddhist centers. As of this writing, Lieb tells me Peter is living in a monastery in Italy. When I asked Peter his plans for the off-season (only hours away), he tells me India, maybe Nepal, a favorite ashram.

By Goat Creek our conversation had become more a subliminal confirmation of shared perspective than an exchange of ideas. During the Battle of the Bulge in WW II, German commandos slipped behind Allied lines, posing as American troops and driving Allied vehicles. When the Allies caught on, they set up roadblocks where they grilled everyone who approached with questions like "Who was Mickey Mouse's girlfriend?" Talking with Peter that afternoon in the cool shadows of the lower canyon was like that, a means of identifying kindred souls.

I might say: "Simple-consciousness is what the animals have, you know. Self-consciousness is the illusion you have of waking up and thinking you're separate from everything."

And Peter might answer: "Yeah, and language originated at that first moment, you know, at that first shift of consciousness, that first *Aha*."

And I might respond: "Then when you finally figure out that nothing is separate from anything and never *could* have been in the first place, you go on to the next stage and end up like the animals again, but different."

We discussed the magical, beguiling nature of reality as we drifted the swift waters of the lower river that afternoon, and I think we were both renewed by the engagement. In a man like Peter Spiers, quite frankly, I find reassurance of my faith in the human race to evolve.

Before long we could see the main-stem Salmon shining through the canyon ahead and talk drifted again to the mundane. Peter ferried us across the broader flow like a ferryman with an outbound Siddhartha. He let me off at the ramp against the far bank, then steered on down to Cache Bar and the takeout. It had been a fine time for all of us that week, I think, journeying together down the Middle Fork. I have never experienced a more pristine, fecund fishery than along this spanking, young river. It's reassuring to know, too, that the canyon, the river, and the well adjusted trout are safely out of reach of the long arm of human aggrandizement for generations to follow.

I watched Peter for several moments before he drifted from sight. I felt envy for the true, bright place Peter was heading. It was still early for that for me, I realized, but felt like an old fool again anyway, with a familiar angst and a touch of the tragic, but decided to wader up again instead, while I waited for the rest of the crew. I did this and rose stiffly, picked up my rod, and hiked along the dusty access road above the now broad, green Salmon River in the building heat of midday, looking for one last trout or two.

Middle Fork

General: *You can do the river on your own, provided you get a permit. Only a certain number are issued each year. Better yet to go with an established outfitter. The river is not unchallenging at all in terms of rapids, either. Unless you are an experienced river-runner and are prepared to take on the 80-odd rapids the river has to offer (and are willing to take the time to scout each major rapid), you are better off with an outfitter. Even for those with experience, this is the kind of river that is best served by floating the first time with an experienced guide. Season runs typically from July through September.*

Most of the licensed commercial outfitters on the Salmon are not focusing exclusively on the fishing. The river is such a full-scope recreational hit that many people run it for its own sake, with the fishing a pleasant diversion. Middle Fork Wilderness Outfitters do have exceptionally knowledgeable fishermen among their ranks and devote several trips each year to a fly fishing theme.

The trout in this area spawn in the tributaries, mostly during the spring. May through June, but it is likely to be the middle of July before you get on the river anyway. Water levels are quite high early in the season, and better fishing conditions develop as the level drops. The salmon fly hatch comes off later here than other western streams; by the time you've got a comfortable water level to float, you'll probably be picking Pteronarcys off your sunburned neck.

The mayfly hatches seem to be scattered over the course of a rather short mountain season. We saw some stately green and gray drakes, but nothing in fishable quantities. Blue-winged olives and sulfurs were the most evident. Blue wings were better a little earlier or later in the day, with sulfurs or Pink Alberts emerging more in the middle.

Caddis come on by midsummer and offer evening action, usually out of camp. They are green, yellow, and tan, mostly, in standard sizes. But it is the grasshopper that carries the day throughout the heart of the season.

Middle Fork hoppers come predominantly in tan, yellow, and light olive. While any one of these may do the trick, I would have all three colors in my book.

The Parachute Hopper, as mentioned, seems to be the favorite not only of fishermen, but of fish as well. I fished my high-floating Sofa Pillows and Stimulators effectively too.

The nymph or larva dropper suspended 12 to 18 inches from a big dry, is a popular and very effective tactic. You can vary the combo to match the emergence of the species, mayfly or caddis. I've always liked the concept of a dropper and this particular combination has a lot of scope.

What to Bring: *The Middle Fork experience does not require much in the way of specialized fly tackle or technique. Your favorite trout rods in #3 to #6 weight will work fine. Tippets of eight to ten ft. from 4X to 6X. Most of the fishing is from a boat or raft and a long rod is an advantage. You'll want waders if you plan to fish out of a boat.*

Your outfitter will provide a complete trip list of equipment, clothing, and gear, but be prepared for cool evenings and possibly days, more likely warm to hot days and cool nights though, depending on time of year. Thunderstorms are fairly common and rain is always a possibility. Pack accordingly.

Information:
Middle Fork Wilderness Outfitters
Gary and Kitty Shelton
P.O. Box 575
Ketchum, ID 83340
(800) 726-0575
E-mail- mfwo@micron.net
Web site www.gorp.com/mfwo

Transport and shuttle:
McCall Air Taxi
McCall, ID 83638
(208) 634-7137

River Rat Shuttle
The Waite Family
P.O. Box 301
Stanley, ID 83278
800-831-8942

Fly tackle:
Lost River Outfitters
171 N. Main Street
Ketchum, ID 83340
(208) 726-1706

Silver Creek Outfitters
Ketchum, ID 83340
(208) 726-5282
E-mail- silvercreek@sunvalley.net

Lodging:
Idaho Country Inn
Julie Heneghan
P.O. Box 659
Sun Valley, ID 83353
800-250-8341
E-mail: premier-resorts@sunvalley.net

Current fishing regs:
Idaho Dept. of Fish and Game
P.O. Box 25
Boise, ID 83707
(208) 334-3700

General info on lodging and services:
Sun Valley/Ketchum Chamber of Commerce
P.O. Box 2420
Sun Valley, ID 83353
800-634-3347

Salmon Chamber of Commerce
P.O. Box 657
Salmon, ID 83467

Current list of guides and outfitters
serving the Middle Fork:
Idaho Outfitters and Guides Association
P.O. Box 95
Boise, ID 83701

River permits & current river regs:
Middle Fork River Ranger
Challis National Forest
Challis, ID 83226
(208) 879-5204

Olympic Steelhead Journal

Photo by Ken Morrish

Upon first seeing the Olympics, Captain John Mears said in 1788, "If that be not where dwell the Gods, it is certainly beautiful enough to be, and I therefore will call it Mt. Olympus."
Climber's Guide to the Olympic Mountains
- Olympic Mountain Rescue Council

It rained and it rained and it rained.
Pooh Bear - *Winnie the Pooh.* A.A. Milne

Appeared originally in *Wild Steelhead & Salmon* titled, "Olympic Silver"

Highway 101 was filled with logging trucks and pick-ups with clever bumper stickers like: *Timber products not available in this town—wipe your ass with a spotted owl* and *Earth first—log the other planets later*. With my own taste in fender literature running more towards: *Make pizza—not war* or *Love 'em and Leave 'em—Catch and Release* I was not anticipating much commiserating with the locals.

Pulsing through the traffic lights of Port Angeles, the highway wound along the Strait of Juan de Fuca where I looked out my truck window over a 20-mile-wide boulevard of intruding sea. Soon the highway swung inland and crossed the Elwha River, where I was reminded of another zealous human oversight. Built just after the turn of the century, with no provision for fish passage, the hydroelectric dam along the river had committed speciocide against the long-flourishing strains of steelhead and salmon cycling into the alpine headwaters of the Elwa watershed. Rolling high over the bridge on the Elwa, I passed into National Forest. Five miles further I came under the aegis of National Parks and skirted Swiss-looking Lake Crescent with its mysterious blue-backed Beardsley trout (really land-locked steelies) that glide through waters so clear you can see a 100 feet down in places. Waterfalls spilled off steepening terrain and whooshed through culverts all along the highway. The impression of both lushness and remoteness built as the highway bowled through distant, rural hamlets, truck stops, and tackle/convenience stores, until even these thinned out finally and nothing remained but timber or stumps, one long two-lane highway, and the many green steel bridges that announced each new river or creek.

A dozen major rivers spiral down from the rare circular mountain range that is the Olympics. Nearly 200 inches of snow and rain brush the peaks in the interior of this rugged country. Rivers with native names like Hoh, and Bogachiel, Sol Duc, and

Duckabush are continually infused; when the rains slow a bit in summer the snow starts to melt, and when the snow's gone the glaciers kick in and take up the slack. I didn't know it at the time, but this coastal mountain fishery would come to remind me of the Norwegian streams I knew of through the writings of Ritz and Schweibert—big fish, bred by big water, and, while the Olympic rivers did not have the gradient of the Aaro, for example, they were powerful, year 'round, hard-flowing rivers descending from steep, glacier-pocked mountains.

"These are the big fellas," Ken told me on the phone several months earlier. "From March on they're nearly all wild fish. Over half of them are 'three-salts.' If you want to have a decent chance of hooking a 20-pound native here in the states, this is the place!"

It was the first week in April. Ken Morrish and Ned Patton had driven north together from southern Oregon, where Ken heads up the Ashland Outdoor Store. Ned motored an earlier leg up from the U.C. Davis campus where he was finishing up a doctorate in atmospheric science. I had traveled south, ferrying much of the distance on the yeoman ferries that shuttle around the Northwest's enormous inland sea.

Both Ken and Ned were experienced, highly motivated fishermen, but to give you an idea just how demanding the Olympic rivers can be, in well over a dozen trips out here, Kenny had hooked only five steelhead (although a photo of one of these brutes had already graced the cover of one fly fishing magazine), while Ned had put in 14 days of diligent fishing without a hook-up! It was my first trip out to the Peninsula, and I had no illusions that it would be easy.

Sitting comfortably that night by the massive rock fireplace in the Eagle Point Inn, nestled on the banks of the upper Sol Duc, we agreed the rivers looked good. We could not hear the rain beating against the roof of the inn, but we could see it dripping over the blackened eaves. Rain was predicted throughout the week and, from what we'd been able to pick up talking with other fishermen that day, fishing had been slow. Dan Christensen, the innkeeper, told us Yvonne Chouinard and Thomas McGuane had stayed with him only a week earlier and had managed only one fish between them in a week of hard fishing.

The immense fir beams and walls of the cabin were like the bones of some enormous beast. We heard nothing that night and slept deeply in plush beds with stuffed rabbits (courtesy of our host) on each of our pillows—totems, I hoped, of the fecundity of the powerful Olympic rivers.

Tripped up by my usual disorganization, I couldn't keep up with the guys next morning and sent them on ahead to the Hungry Bear Cafe, grub spot and watering hole for loggers and fishermen alike, to rendezvous with Dave Steinbaugh, our guide for the day. Just as I was finally ready to roll, they drove up. Ken and Ned got out of truck and came around and looked at me. Ken grinned and said, "Good thing you didn't show up looking like that."

"How's that?" I answered.

He pointed at my legs, where I had on my trusty pile tights, a second skin I practically lived in throughout the winter months.

"And that," he said, pointing at my jacket. "They wouldn't like that pink jacket none either."

"It's fuschia," I told him. "And who the hell are they?"

"While we were having breakfast with Dave," Ken explained, "I told him I was anxious for him to meet you, that you were your own man and all, and dressed a little differently, when you bothered to dress at all—I told him to watch the reaction of the loggers at the counter when you came in. He wanted to know why, and I told him you'd probably show up wearing tights.

Photo by Ken Morrish

Dave Steinbaugh about to release Ken's fish.

'Ooooooooooo,' Steinbaugh moaned ominously. "That's not good."

"These guys don't see a lot of that around here you know, and when they do, well…they don't like it."

We had a huge laugh at this, especially at the "well…they don't like it" part, but I bristled all week at the bias.

Our first full day of fishing the Peninsula dawned cool and clear. An hour after sunrise we were ferrying across the lower Bogachiel to get first water on some of Dave's favorite beats. Unlike on the Sol Duc, you could get around here pretty well, and the anatomy of the holding water and traveling routes was more evident. Broad sand beaches and gravel bars swung from one side of the river to the other; channels, flats, and riffle lines were cleanly defined. Before long I could see Dave trailing down toward Ned and myself; he told us Ken had landed one already several hundred yards above us, a 33-inch, 13–14-pound native! We were feeling pretty good about that and leaned into our work with a relish for several hours more but had no further luck.

"It's a tricky bit of water to float." Dave briefed us on the extreme upper Sol Duc, where we were headed that noon. "And it might be dicey from time to time with the four of us in the boat, but I think it might be our best chance to get into some fish." As we pulled off on the shoulder of the highway, the sun was shining through the trees and the air was warm. Launch was a vertical, 15-foot drop over a clay bank that Steinbaugh gently winched the dory over until we caught it from below. I noticed an old fellow sitting back against a tree eating his lunch and walked over to say hello. He reminded me of the Gump. He was retired, he told me, lived nearby and was taking his lunch by the river. We chatted while the guys shuttled our rig down river.

He told me about his latest visits to the river and a big steel-head he'd recently caught. Senile or simpleton, I couldn't quite tell but, listening to the man talk of fishing the day before and of going out for halibut the next weekend, I knew he was the real pagoda; he reminded me of myself and my friends as kids, of that simple, threshold passion we had for fishing. I suspected he did not bother with a fly rod, nor cared little about such things as high-tech equipment or sophisticated technique. My hit was that this man's life, unlike most of our own with the onset of 'matu-rity,' was still rooted in that self-sustaining, bliss-like paradise of the feeble-minded and the fisher-youth—a place or state, I think, that most of us worked like devils to reclaim. I felt some genuine homage for this old fellow and, as we cut loose from the bank, I looked up and he was smiling big and waving hard, both of which I returned in kind.

One of us was always up flicking a fly through each oily look-ing lick of pocket, roily run, and glassy flat we passed, usually two of us, bow and stern, our eyes boring underwater for mercu-rial shapes, our flies darting over the dancing water like dragon-flies, then sinking as little bits of steel trailing feather and hair. Between the frequent boulder fields that Steinbaugh masterfully negotiated and the numerous steelies we flushed or fished to (those few on the redds we left alone), it was a memorable float. Defi-nitely, the fish were home; getting them to take was the chal-lenge. Water temperature was mid-to-upper forties, not so cold as to prevent fish from chasing our flies. *This is quite simply the way of winter steelheading*, I reminded myself.

"Steelhead come into these rivers 12 months of the year," Steinbaugh told us as he maneuvered the boat. "Most of the fish-ing pressure is for the fall salmon and spring steelhead. The win-ter fish will start coming in November, and of those rivers with a hatchery run it'll be from November to January, then after that February, March or April the vast majority of fish you catch will be wild fish, if not exclusively wild fish. The best steelheading is when the big natives are in. Most of them are at least two salts. Average size 12-pounds, with 25-pound fish not uncommon at all. If you know the water, I think these rivers are much higher percentage than the Seattle rivers. There's a healthier run of wild fish on these rivers here than anywhere else in the states."

There is a lushness to the western Peninsula. Birth and death are interwoven themes across a forest floor of nurse logs and seedlings. A magnificent, endangered ecosystem, the temperate rain forest originally occupied only an infinitesimal *one fifth of one percent* of the earth's surface. Rivers glint like veins of dark ore under brooding skies, or on occasion, like that afternoon, of brightest silver. Dave was right about the upper. Some of it was challenging to negotiate with four men aboard. Boulder fields were the name of the game so high in the watershed, and many of the steepest gradients, where obstacles are typically swept into the deeper pools below, remained studded with rock. I had the impression we were the shiny metal ball in a pinball machine. Ken told me later that he had never before floated with a finer boatman.

The bottom was colored like a bowl of Trix; leaning over the gunwale, I stared down through the slick in the shadow of the hull, mesmerized by the streaming colors. Fishing a Spey rod, Ken worked the river well; Steinbaugh fished the long rod like a wizard, though, swinging dark, bunny matukas and bright, Glasso-inspired speys through the crystal waters with the panache of a skilled veteran. Dave's fly book lay beside his seat; I picked it up and looked inside. The flies were neat, uniform and extraordinarily well tied. Dave told us he'd been tying for over 25 years and was just in the process of opening a mail-order fly and materials company to go with his guiding operation. I asked him about the patterns he fished most here.

"I like to fish larger flies most of the time, unless the water is really low," he told me, "rabbit strip flies in black or hot orange, hot pink, red. The General Practitioner is always a good one, and different kinds of Spey flies—black speys, bright orange speys, the traditional speys from when Glasso used to fish out here. The Sol Duc series. We fish chrome-eyed rabbit strip flies too. Sometimes big marabou spiders and other big shrimpy flies that we'll fish on up to three, four, even 5/0 hooks, even on a floater or lighter sinking line in certain water depths."

From time to time we passed a thin riparian zone and glimpsed the devastation looming behind. We'd seen no other boats along this stretch, and only moderate pressure on the lower river as yet. I asked Dave if this was the norm? "Crowding can be a problem along certain stretches of rivers at times," he said, "if you're trying to compete as a fly fishermen with other boats on the river that are pulling plugs or casting bait. Even though you *can* get away from them and still do real well."

We fished with a building imminency that afternoon, but only our eyes connected with steelhead, 20 or more we calculated later, and some of them pushing 20 pounds.

Syd Glasso is the old man of these Olympic rivers. School teacher by day, avant-garde fly tier by night. Best known for his exquisitely tied Spey flies (the Heron and the Sol Duc series in particular), Glasso and his protégé, Dick Worthington, baptized many a gorgeous new pattern in tumbling rain forest waters. Adapted from the drab but seductive patterns of the River Spey and the River Dee of northern Scotland, Glasso's versions are dressed with brighter materials. It is the rare steelhead fly tier

Photo by Ken Morrish

Photo by Author on Fujifilm

nowadays who hasn't been influenced by Glasso's work.

While the Skykomish, the Stillaguamish, and the Skagit were home streams for some of the northwest's fly fishing greats—Ralph Wahl, Harry Lemire, and Les Johnson among the notable—the rivers of the Peninsula were as darkest Africa not so many years ago. Seattle rivers were generally convenient day fisheries, while a visit to the Peninsula was inherently more of an undertaking. For all its majesty and big native steelhead, the Peninsula had a dearth of fishing legends associated with it. I asked Dave if this might just be because of the remoteness.

"Everybody has seemed to come out here and fish at one time or another," he told me, "but they haven't spent a lot of time, for whatever reason. I think it *is* primarily because of the remoteness. I think, though, if you're going to come out to try and learn the rivers here, you're either going to have to pick a river and try and learn that river as well as you can, or just try and pick a few spots and get to know those spots well. If you try and jump from river to river, it'll take a lot more time to learn. There's so much variety here that you can fish a different piece of water each trip. Which is an advantage, really. You just have to put in your time."

Two days later we had moved from the comfort of the inn to Three Rivers Resort and a rustic little cabin situated at the juncture of the Sol Duc and Bogachiel rivers. To date, the only fish we'd tied into was Kenny's, our first day. Lack of sleep was starting to show on me, although I'd been able to catnap a little. The rains settled in with us at the cabin. Situated at the confluence of the two rivers, the resort was built in an extremely versatile location, and with a cafe and gas pumps, tackle and grocery store, it was a veritable hub for the sparsely populated area. We would fish in the morning with Kurt Ingram, our host.

Sandwiches for lunch that afternoon as we tracked up the linoleum floor with muddy wading boots, but the respite was sorely needed. And as a little Frisbee golf is as good as napping for true aficionados, Ken and I sketched out an impromptu course around the cabins. Ned sat glumly on the front steps. I couldn't believe it! Ned was Frisbee golf gonzo on the Davis campus but he sat on the porch outside the door in an icy glum. Obviously peeved that we'd take time out for recreation other than fishing, he announced flatly, "No way, man. I came to fish." Ned would have none of our diversion, and in the end we shot only a token three holes under rain-blackened maples and piled back into the truck.

Without the benefit of a drift boat, we'd been bushwhacking and hoofing major sections of waterfront. I had the impression that peninsula roads don't so much parallel rivers as abut them obliquely. If you're not fishing around one of the bridges, you're at the mercy of a maze of logging roads, many without signs, that seem to provide the majority of river access. Parked at the end of an abandoned logging spur littered with decaying couches and a bullet-pocked washing machine, we were confronted by a dreary-looking scene but, when I looked up, a pair of bald eagles were soaring above the swaying trees.

Tunneling through a grove of nascent-leafed alders to the lower Duc, we came out finally on a braided mix of gravel bars and islands with some exciting-looking channels swirling between. Winding through forest and farmland up only a few miles from its confluence with the Bogie, the river had quickness still, but also maturity; the gradient was less and the earmarks of excess made channels and holes better defined, and getting around on shoals and gravel bars and beaches was much easier than the jumbled rawness of the upper river.

Ned had a huge pull right off upstream; I heard him yelp. The stage we were at, any such nip, pluck, bump, strike or touch was grounds for spirited yodeling. He told me about it as he came leap-frogging downriver, after a while past me, where I sat on the bank with my feet in the water changing back over from a 200-grain sink-tip to a floater.

I had fished the big rod and sinking line for several days until my wrist was about to go carpal. I knew I could catch fish on a dry line on almost any river under optimum conditions. I knew too that, with high water and stubborn fish, we were better off swinging deeply sunk flies laterally across the breadth of the channel than down linear, dead-drifted routes or on top water swings. Still, like the drunk looking for his wallet under the streetlight, I would see what I could find.

I scoured the channels and tail-outs with a pair of flies, a heavy black nymph on the dropper and a favorite summer pattern, a sleekly tied Mack's Canyon improv on point. The water was just delicious. Ticking flies through the deepest channels and swinging them up hard at the tail, I realized again that, after many years of fishing where hooking summer steelhead was a regular occurrence, I had developed a persistent sense of anticipation. A very pleasant state of being too, after so many years of anguishing over fishing objectives. It seemed, also, that there was a temporal period of efficacy, like a tetanus shot, before the end of which a booster of flush fishing was required to maintain the condition. During this time, though, I seemed to be fully inoculated.

Undisturbed in my reverie by any flesh-and-blood quarry, I dwelt on the enigma that is running water. Watching it, I imagined trying to describe it to someone who had never seen it—an old rumination of mine. *And the river bed, she was dry and crone-like when abandoned, but wet, form-shaping and in dynamic balance with her dark lover moving heavily upon her.* Meditating thusly, and working the water meanwhile quite thoroughly, I came up zip. Wading across the river, I climbed a steep bank on a well-worn, brown clay trail that dipped under a farmer's fence, then skirted the edge of his large tilled field running in a 30-foot crescent along a hundred yards of riverbank. The biggest maple trees I'd ever seen ringed that bluff.

The Peninsula has been Logging Central for generations of rugged woodsmen living in the dense rain forests, but winds of change were soughing through the remaining trees. Recently I'd traveled the entire western coast of Vancouver Island by kayak and seen the damage first-hand to the belt of rivers and giant trees that extended south from the Olympics into Northern Cal, and north into southern Alaska. The temperate rain forest is truly logging paradise; old growth trees are huge, straight-grained and exceptionally dense, but restraint was sorely needed to sustain not only the remaining old growth forest, but the unique biosystem that flourishes there. Besides the concern over the endangered spotted owl and marbled murrelet, the wild steelhead and salmon that spend their early life in forest streams are the tragic victims of careless cutting. Where there are trees as lush as yak's hair there are rivers, and where there are rivers, there are fish… in this case, a number of tremendous runs of wild fish that had long lived in harmony with indigenous peoples before the onslaught of Western aggrandizement. And, though many of the native strains are extant today, they are nevertheless only a shadow of their former presence.

Below me was Syd's run; I watched Ned fishing it. A classic swing run, it looked to me like it would fish better in lower water. Ned worked the run like a dog on point . . . "tight" was the word that came to mind. For this guy, it was all tightly focused energy and low, tightly cannoned loops. As the rains resumed, I got up stiffly and headed down the high bluff, scoping the water.

Besides getting up to speed with these powerful rivers and trying like the devil to put flies in bony mouths, we were all making our peace with the rain. Only dry at night when we spilled

A drift boat floating the final leg to take-out at twilight.

A fine Bogie hen.

Photo by Ken Morrish

Ken with a large Bogie fish.

into our lodging like muskrats and steamed up the windows with racks of wet gear, nowhere had I ever felt it more tangibly, this ever-present cycle of moisture—river, rain, sweat, things I drank and things I showered in. I could feel it running down my neck and nose and dripping onto my shoulders, feel it pushing against my legs and absorbed into my wrinkled, dish-pan hands. I could only trust it was evaporating somewhere else. Later, at the cabin, I had a cup of tea and a hot shower. Warmth was our operating threshold now, wetness a given.

We had yet to hook another fish since Ken's fish that first day, but certainly not from lack of trying. The fish were there; we knew that for a fact. A good many of them had been covered too; we had no doubt about that, either. Each of us dealt with our unrequited efforts differently, I noticed. If there was one word to describe Ken Morrish, it was *irrepressible*, always upbeat, and like the heron, always on the *qui vive* for fish. Ned, on the other hand, entered the water with the grim determination and tenacity of one of Tolkein's legendary dwarves.

I, under the circumstances, exhibited a bit less doggedness than my hard-bitten friends. While struggling to adjust to winter tackle and deep fly swings, I was nevertheless intently focused on each cast, fishing with steady anticipation, and happy enough, as that's what sautéed my fillet anyway. Why the fish were nixing us, though, no one knew.

As we drove back to the cabin at dusk, rain pelted the windshield. Fatigued from long days and short nights, my attention defaulted to the rhythmic sweep of the wiper blades. When I glanced at the other guys I could see the glazed look to their eyes, too. Thinking back on Syd's run I remembered it was there that Syd had taken his then-world-record, 18-pound fish. Connected to that was the memory of Ken's first Sol Duc fish that was the image of Syd's. I had not yet heard the full story, so I asked Ken to tell us.

"It was the first fish I ever landed on the Sol Duc," he said, his eyes brightening, "and I never expect to land a lower forty-eight fish that large again. It was at the pool that Ned and I had named the Big Flat Pool, which in hindsight was a poor name for such an interesting piece of water. I had fished several of the beat's downstream holes half a dozen times before and, though I had never seen much happen there, it was one of my favorite spots within the body of the bigger run. We call this particular beat 'The Thrash,' because of the severity of the bushwhacking you have to undergo to get into it."

"A major bitch," Ned confirmed. "Makes the bushwhack we just made look like a stroll."

"My dad and I had fought our way in from upriver this time, and it was still very early when I left him fishing the upper section of the run and thrashed my way down to the pool. The rocks were still covered in frost and a gentle mist was rising from the river. I knew the part of the pool that I wanted to fish first and stupidly barged right out into the head of it, only to find the water higher and stronger than before. Even before I'd finished stripping line for the first cast, I lost my footing and shipped a bunch of water, then scuttled back to the bank to regroup. A little disappointed, I settled into fishing the bend's shallower, slower inside. On the fourth or fifth cast, my line grew tight; as I set, I was fairly certain it was a fish. For the first few minutes the fish stayed in the pool, swimming sullenly around the bottom; I knew it was good sized but could not get a gauge in absolute terms. Then a few minutes later it rolled and showed the red flank of a buck. I still hadn't seen enough of it yet, though, to make a call on its actual size.

"I was hollering for Bill to come down, thinking I had a beautifully colored 10- or 12-pound buck and wanted him to get a few pictures. Eventually he showed up, panting and looking somewhat worse for the wear; he'd been worried that I might be drowning. With the fish showing no initiative, I started putting the screws to it. That's when the light went on. There I was reefing with my nine-and-a-half eight weight and the thing wasn't budging at all. The big rod felt suddenly small and soft. The fish made several doggy, uninspired runs around the pool and both Bill and I started to wonder what I'd tied into. But after about ten minutes the fish began to tire and circled slowly within my reach. Only when I finally grabbed its wrist and cradled its heavy body in my hands, did we realize the immensity of it. He was double striped, over three feet long, and about 19 inches in girth. And check this out: opposite from my fly, which was just barely hanging from a flap of skin on the inside of its upper jaw, was a three-foot section of frayed 15-pound Maxima and a barbed, well-buried, 2/0 Gamagatsu!"

Back at the cabin, rain parkas, vests, gloves, waders and wool caps hung over the back of the kitchen chairs and on hangers from the ceiling vent over the gas heater to dry, we hoped, before morning. Anyway, it didn't seem to matter much, anymore, the rain becoming like a stray dog we had finally adopted. Ned, of course, was the rain man. To put the trip onto a scientific footing, he turned on the porch light and opened the door. A sheet of water cascaded off the roof onto our front steps: "'R' minus is light rain, 'R' is a steady rain, and this stuff," he said, with an impish grin as he stuck his hand through the waterfall, "is an 'R'+."

Bobby Kearsey is compact in his hugeness, bearded, clean-cut, and unmistakably friendly looking. A fishing guide compatriot of Ken's in Alaska, he had found us somehow out in the sticks. Like a contented bear, Bobby settled quickly into fine humor in our cabin that night. We ordered take-out from a Chinese restaurant in Forks and, while Ned drove off to get it, we started the poker game. Kurt Ingraham came down that night to visit and to make arrangements for the morning and talked our ears off about fishing; we were left a little stunned by the monologue. We resumed the game afterward as the rain pelted us with a vengeance and had us worrying that everything might be blown in the morning. About midnight, just for emphasis, it turned to hail, and beat against the metal roof like plastic bullets.

Big fish were no rare occurrence on the Peninsula; both Ken and Kurt had made that quite clear, as had the grisly photos in evidence in every little market and tackle shop we'd visited. The peninsula had big fish in good numbers, but it was also the standard, as it turned out, by which a number of other things were measured. I couldn't remember another destination with such a cluttered mantle.

The Peninsula is a land of enormous trees. The largest specimen of Alaska cedar lives here. The world's largest grand fir, and the western hemlock *patronne*, even two of the world's buffest Doug firs are locals. I figure that's about like a college football team having the Heisman *and* the Lombardi trophy winners on its team together. Furthermore, the rain forests along the Washington coast are veritable *organic black holes,* where the fecundity of life and its nourishment—the biosystem—is literally both the *densest* and *heaviest* in the known world.

This largess extends even to the political realm, whereby the immense Olympic National Park (at nearly a million acres) is one of the largest tracts of wilderness left in the contiguous states. It is also a World Heritage Site, and the National Seashore that parallels much of the park is one of the longest continuous stretches of wild coastline in, again, the continental forty-eight. That the many great rivers here have such healthy numbers of large wild steelhead is largely a function of place.

Floating the upper Sol Duc. Ken in front, Dave at the oars, author in stern.

Ned, hard at it in typical "R" ish conditions.

Rather articulate sign along one stretch of the Sol Duc.

Next morning the asphalt was deeply puddled and the R-plus was in fine form. We were up at five o'clock, though, ducking out from under the waterfall and wandering through the dark and the downpour between the cafe that Kurt had opened for us, where he was brewing lattes, and the cabin where we touched up leaders, flies, and lines, and tried to stay regular. Ned was foaming at the delays in getting on stream until, finally, several hours later, we were underway.

A short drive to the confluence told us it was only the Duc that was fishable that day and, by the color of the water, maybe only the extreme upper Duc at that. After driving around in the mountains in a rainstorm for over an hour, we were above the chocolate, finally, but the river was still murky. It looked good enough to us who were past ready to fish, though, and we filed out with our waders on and started sliding our rods out of the back of Kurt's new van.

Kurt rummaged in the van a while, then walked back to where we were rigged up and stuffing energy bars and spare lenses into the back of our vests. With a strange, even countenance he said, "I don't know how to tell you guys this…" and there was a long pause and a pained look in his eyes. It felt to me as though he were going to confess some dark secret, or maybe tell us we had offended him somehow without knowing it. I was relieved to hear him announce only that he had forgotten his waders.

Up the trail a short distance, a chunk of river split around a couple of boulders and formed two distinct channels of flow. The river was gorgeous here, smaller, rawer, and wilder-looking among towering conifers and stubbly clear cuts. I fished down through both the channels feeling like a million bucks, sinking a big marabou spey deeply into the quick currents, fishing a short length of tip and a short tag of leader and getting it right down—boom, boom, boom—imagining a big native buck slapping me silly at any moment. An hour or so later I saw Ken and Ned upstream, trooping down, knee deep over a gravel bar together and they were fishless as well. Kurt showed up about then with his waders, and we fished another length more. But the rain continued pounding; the water inexorably turning. Half an hour later we were all fishing the biggest, brightest patterns we had, then the rain turned up a notch and the river was gone.

Ned was a hard guy to figure. I admired his Ahab-like ability to stay on track, especially given his current string of luck, but I found the behavior just a bit maniacal. In the end, I would come to understand that this was a guy who, with a great sense of humor and an extraordinary ability to focus, had gotten himself a PhD at the ripe old age of 28, while somehow managing to fish constantly: New Zealand, the Babine, the Umpqua and, most of all, his home streams in the Sierras—the McCloud, the Yuba, the Sac and others. The message on his answering machine said it all: "Hi, I'm either at work or out fishin' —leave a message." It occurred to me too that, for all Ned's inner angst about his luck on the Peninsula, I could not remember seeing him down when he was fishing. Always, on the water he was absorbed; if you broke through to him, you'd get a smile likely as not, and there was no half-heartedness, no aura of defeat about the man.

We headed to the upper Duc again after lunch with two kayaks strapped to our rack. We dragged them easily over the salal, ferns, and moss to the river. The boats were made by Ocean Kayaks, a local Washington company, open on top, easy on and off, unlike conventional style kayaks. We stuck our rods and vests inside the fuselages and scooted across the river to fish the far shore. We drifted stretches where we could haul the kayaks out again to the highway. Even with the steady rains, the water was holding its visibility well enough, although it was higher than ideal. But still, nothing.

We headed to the Pump-House Hole next, and the rain had thinned to a mist. Standing on a steep, grassy bank, we could see fish holding in a fine, long, steady run below the bank. Encouraged, we took turns casting to them and spotting from the bank. An exciting change of pace this, and the sun made an unscheduled appearance for an hour or so. Ken and Ned were back in New Zealand together drifting flies from crouched positions to sullen fish, while I drifted off alone to try my luck.

Fewer fishable runs appeared beside the trail as I headed upstream to scout the river. As I hiked along, I became aware of the larger scale of things... in my mind's eye I could see the engorged sponge that is the rain forest shuttling water like a band of partisans across the forest floor to the conduits of clean-rocked rivers and blending, finally, into salt. Then, out of the corner of my eye, I spotted a fish rolling against the far bank.

I dropped a 2/0 bastard spey well upstream of the rise and dead drifted it past where I suspected the fish was holding. A dozen times or so. Then I waded upstream in strong current so I could lift it in front of that spot. I covered all around the lick where he breached feeling renewed anticipation purely from the sighting, then finally gave up and spent another hour exploring further up river.

Rendezvousing back at the truck, we hoped each other had the news, but no, still no fish, not so much as a strike. Again, we had seen plenty below the pump house, some moving, some holding, but just could not entice one to strike. Ken told me Bobby had decided to return to Seattle that night instead of staying over another day. Kurt had obligations to attend to and wished us luck. I like this Kurt, I decided. A bit of a talker, he was also generous, bright, friendly. And ardent, definitely... fly fishing was high passion for the man.

Dusk. A winding gravel road carried a short distance through dense forest then broke out in view of an old homesite situated beside the river. The Bogachiel came up alongside the road like a host and led us neatly around to our last digs of the trip. The Brightwater House loomed invitingly out of the mist and had me feeling a bit like Bilbo approaching the sanctuary of Elrond's Last Homely House.

In the gathered dull light of a rain-streaked sunset, I was feeling sated from a week's hard-waged efforts, a subtle thing, though, unlike the heady flush of success (but then *subtle*, I was realizing more and more, seemed to come hand-in-hand with the graying of beards). As we approached the old homestead site, we noticed a herd of enormous elk grazing like phantoms in the orchard.

"Puts new meaning into 'home river', eh?" I remarked, as we got out and watched a guide in a drift boat pulling hard against the black water, while a fisherman standing in the bow arced a spoon into the deepening dusk. Looking pretty ratty, we went inside to meet more new faces.

Settled into the upstairs bedrooms, I felt more like one of the Chesmore's kids coming home from college than a stranger staying the night. After a week of standing in rivers and under dripping or gushing skies, hiking through wet branches and bushes, water inside my waders and everything soaked, we took quick showers, stashed our gear upstairs, and came down to join the party. We were all feeling pretty darned good; it was our last night on the Peninsula, and we'd been invited to a dinner party.

Like fools lured in out of the rain (our hair was still wet, at least), we wandered through the house snacking on hors d'oeuvres, drinking huge mugs of beer, and chatting with the other guests. Richard and Beth Chesmore had invited a local guide, Bob Piggot, his wife Pat, and a fly fishing artist named Jack Datisman. Bob had been instrumental in getting some prime and fragile areas of

the Sol Duc set aside as "fly only" water. Richard was an archae-
ologist by trade and a regular on the local streams. At the dinner
table that night there was excited talk of fishing the Peninsula
rivers, and both Ken and Piggot were animated in praise of the
spey rod.

I had watched these guys fishing spey rods all week. While
the efficacy of a 15-foot fly rod as a pure fishing tool is a given,
and the graceful, powerful stroke of the rod is a small perfor-
mance in itself, I had decided that the big rod was just not for me.
Not simply for the sake of minimalism—no one could accuse me
of that—but because the light rod, the wand, was the sweetest
way I knew how to fish. Admittedly, it was tougher setting up
well in fast, high water, stacking a pile of tight mends just above
a 300-grain tip. I was lost to such musings that night while talk
flew all around me; I felt spent after a week's hard efforts, and
indulged in a bit of pleasant introversion at a table with half a
dozen other inspired conversationalists.

Beth had made us a delicious lasagna that was rich and warm
and the perfect antidote for soggy souls, the plentiful wine acting
like a sheep-dog, steering conversation from one fertile pasture
to the next.

Soft-spoken, talented, local fly fishing artist Datisman had won
several national awards. His handiwork appeared on Steinbaugh's
card and on the cover of his new mail-order fly catalog (and six
months later, on Ken's business card as well). Jack's work were
trademark bucks, large and mean, and hens, plump and sexy looking… fish with personality.

The night was easy, providential, the wine and beer copious.
While we tackled homemade pie for dessert, talk swung again to
the challenge of fishing the Peninsula rivers. Considering Ned
was zero for 20 days running, that Ken's ratio was about the same,
and that I had not even had a strike this week, *challenge* was pure
euphemism.

"Hey," Piggot said. "I don't care if I have the best steelhead fly fisher in the world in my boat, we can still go four straight without touching a fish!"

Ken said, "You know, even if I haven't caught many fish here, it's rivers like the Sol Duc that make it all worthwhile. That's got to be my favorite all-time stream, the way the surreal colors spring up from its cobbled, mosaic bottom . . . and how the alders and maples, heavy with moss, reach down in longing for the river. I love the raw, rough purity of it all."

It doesn't hurt either, I thought, *to throw in the occasional 18-pound reward. It was a beautiful place to hang, all right, but it transforms a nature hike into a saga when you hook a steelhead as big as a yearling pig.*

I'd been watching Piggot during Ken's eulogy and thought I could sense his surprise that a young, visiting fisherman from southern Oregon could describe a Peninsula river in such a way that all he needed to do was to smile softly and nod in conspiracy as though he, himself, had just spoken.

To bask in the comfort of society after a week in the rain had been a welcome event, a kind of primal swooning into the tissue of humanity. Certainly, it would have been fine also to have hooked some of the big fresh-run steelhead that the Peninsula is known for. *But otherwise,* I thought, *the party was a perfect ending to this trip* and, lifting my wine glass, I managed a few words, at least, to that. In bed late, I fell asleep to the sounds of the river outside my open window running softly through the night and the rain guttering onto the patio deck.

After returning home, I kept in touch with Steinbaugh. He apprised me of the latest developments in the on-going struggle over native steelhead on Peninsula rivers. During February of '96, Washington's Fish and Wildlife Commission met and declared

Photo by Ken Morrish

Author, high-stickin' on the upper Sol Duc.

an intention to implement further protection for wild steelhead on the Peninsula. Instead of the current 30-fish annual harvest quota, the Commision was planning a major reduction to two wild fish annually in the Sol Duc, Bogachiel, Calawah, and Hoh. In addition, they would introduce Wild Steelhead Release regs like those currently in effect on the upper Sol Duc, to sections of the aforementioned streams, as well as the entire Clearwater.

After further input and much controversy later that spring, however, the Commission compromised its earlier position. Although a major reduction in wild fish harvest quotas of five would be implemented, the single, barbless, no bait (WSR) regulations they had intended for some Peninsula rivers were dropped.

While this was a bitter pill for those following the roller coaster proceedings to have to swallow, it could, of course, have fared worse. Exasperated with heel-dragging progress toward outright protection of all native steelhead stocks, in his most recent conversation with me Dave summed up not only the wild steelhead dilemma on the Peninsula, but the entire contemporary human relationship to wild species: "The thing is," he said, "it would be a lot smarter to implement the changes now, you know, before the catastrophe, instead of after, like we usually do."

Amen.

Olympic Peninsula

Resources:

Info and Maps:
North Olympic Peninsula
Visitor and Convention Bureau

> *Main Office*
> *P.O. Box 670*
> *338 W. 1st, Suite 104*
> *Port Angeles, WA 98362*
> *1-800-942-4042*

> *Field Office*
> *P.O. Box 1442*
> *Forks Visitor Center*
> *Forks, WA 98331*
> *(360) 374-9845*

Olympic National Park
600 E. Park
Pt. Angeles, WA 98362
(360) 452-4501 Ext: 230

U.S. Forest Service/National Park Service
Information Centers
Five miles north of Forks on Hwy # 101
(360) 374-6522

Washington State Dept. of Fisheries
115 General Ad. Building
Olympia, WA 98504

Washington State Tourism
Map and Directory
800-544-1800

Guiding, fly fishing:
Waters West
Dave Steinbaugh
Guide service, materials and flies

P.O. Box 3241
Port Angeles, WA 98362
(October thru mid-May)
(360) 417-0937

Lodging:

Eagle Point Inn
Chris and Dan Christensen
P.O. Box 546
Beaver, WA 98305
(360) 327-3236

Three Rivers Resort
Kurt Ingraham
Guiding, cabins, food, and tackle
7764 La Push Road
Forks, WA 98331
(360) 374-5300

Brightwater House B&B
Richard and Beth Chesmore
440 Brightwater Drive
Forks, WA 98331
(360) 374-5453

Elk Meadows B&B
Joe & Joy Baisch
3485 Dosewallips Road
Brinnon, WA 98320
(360) 796-4886

Seaside Lodging:

Straitside Resort
Linda Palumbo
241 Front Street
Sekiu, WA 98381
(360) 963-2100

Juan de Fuca Cottages
Shiela Ramus
182 Marine Drive
Sequim, WA 98382
(360) 683-4433

Big Beaver Valley

Photo by Author on Fujifilm

Now I was beginning to see the Cascades on the northeast horizon, unbelievable jags and twisted rock and snow-covered immensities, enough to make you gulp.

Dharma Bums - Jack Kerouac

Appeared originally in *Fly Rod & Reel*

Tom Barnett, at Ross Lake Resort, had a lot of superlatives for the Beaver Valley when he got me on the phone last summer. "Got a forest of cedar up there dates back to when Constantinople was still the cultural center of the world. There's cougars, wolverines and grizzly bears."

But, what he was most excited about were the trout.

"Creek's been closed forever," he told me, "until two years ago, and there's beaver ponds full of Montana black-spotted cutthroat. We can pack in some kick-boats and fish the ponds, then float the creek back down to the lake. There's some bushwhacking and a couple of portages involved, but I think you guys are gonna want to check this out." With that, he penciled three days on his calendar—September 21, 22, 23—and I penciled them on mine.

Now I was really in mountain country, was how Jack Kerouac had put it, hitching into these North Cascade Mountains for the first time. *The fellows who picked me up were loggers, uranium prospectors, farmers, they drove me through the final big town of Skagit Valley, Sedro Wooley, a farming market town, and then out as the road got narrower and more curved among cliffs and the Skagit River, which we'd crossed on 99 as a dreaming belly river with meadows on both sides, was now a pure torrent of melted snow.*

Steve Thomsen, Ken Morrish, and I were driving up the Skagit ourselves one weekday in the fall of '95, eager to accept Tom's hospitality and bivouac in the comfort of his cabins on the lake. In Jack's day, the Skagit Highway petered out at Marblemount. Not until 1972 had anyone finally managed to punch a road over this forbidding northern range of glacier-scoured valleys, impenetrable moraines, and ragged ridge lines. Even now, it is put to bed by winter storms fully half the year. Names like Mt. Despair,

Mt. Fury, Damnation Creek, Phantom Pass, Big and Little Devil Mountains, Mt. Terror, Desolation Peak, and Nightmare Camp suggest the state of mind the North Cascades induced in early explorers. One summer Kerouac was assigned to Desolation as a fire lookout. His beat prose style best captured the paradox of this awesome country—the corporeal and the sublime. In the midst of these rugged mountains lies the Big Beaver Valley.

The three of us lounged on the bow deck of the Diablo II in the tepid midday sun. Built in the forties to transport visitors and workers to the foot of Ross Dam, the Diablo II motored serenely across the gray-green Diablo Reservoir and entered a narrow fissure at the base of Ruby Mountain. Shafts of light penetrated the cool mountain air. Fir trees, big pines, and occasional maples covered the rocky slopes to the the water's edge. Needles and yellow leaves dusted the surface of the lake. Autumn was in the air, all right, winter right around the corner, and the boat carried, besides ourselves, only two older couples.

We unloaded our gear onto a small dock anchored to a utility area along the base of Ross Dam and waited for the shuttle. A few minutes later an old Chevy flatbed growled down the steep switchbacks to meet us. We threw our gear aboard and climbed onto bench seats running along the side of the bed in the open air and motored slowly toward the lake some 600-feet above. Sunlight filtered down through lodgepole pine, the air redolent with the tree's scent. We passed through several rock tunnels, blasted through mountain flanks. We pulled up, finally, to a small floating dock along the lake, and the vision of white-capped peaks shimmering in miles of blue ice water was stunning. In the distance across the water we could see a string of cabins floating at the base of Sourdough Mountain. Growing quickly larger, Barnett speeds toward us in his sporty mahogany runabout.

The rustic cabins of the resort convey a friendly, relaxed at-

Photo by Ken Morrish

The floating cabins of Ross Lake Resort. Jack Mtn. in background.

Photo by Author on Fujifilm

Tom Barnett.

Photo by Author on Fujifilm

Steve, bushwhacking into the beaver ponds.

Photo by Author on Fujifilm

*Steve, fording the Beaver. Getting to the ponds is a bit of an expedition,
not to mention floating back down the creek.*

mosphere; what's more, they are the only concession on the lake. Standing on deck, you feel the gentle rocking of the floating log raft while your eyes drift up to the surrounding ridgelines and peaks. Tom's love for this lake and surrounding wilderness brought him here to work as a teenager many years ago. Now a part-owner, he cares for the string of old loggers' cabins, remodeling and adding on from a modern woodshop tethered to one end of the resort. As shadows lengthened on the lake, Tom loaned us a boat and we went out to try our luck.

Ross rainbow are likely the descendants of the prince of anadromous fishes, the summer steelhead. Before it was damned in the '20s the Skagit was the Northwest's largest anadromous highway, second only to the mighty Columbia. I talked with Jim Johnston, the regional biologist for Ross: "Summers, you see," he said, "typically are the most likely of the steelhead to produce progeny, some of which don't go to sea. They residualize and become resident. I have no populations of resident rainbow in my area, or any other area that I'm aware of, that did not originate from an anadromous fish. And that is most likley going to be the summer steelhead."

Ross is primarily a trolling lake, and pulling "pop gear" is the prevailing technique, although trolling a single unweighted fly across the surface usually served us well. Because of the extreme draw-down of the water level in the winter for power, there is not much diversity to the insect population. We had always found a hatch of chironomidae, though, emerging at dusk. We let Ken out on Cougar Island, and Steve and I motored over to a nearby bay.

Standing on the bow deck, I could see the calm water ahead of the boat was boiling with fish! The trout appeared to be feeding on rising pupae, as there was no sign of a break in the surface film, only the ubiquitous dimpling. Steve cut the engine, but with an eerie natural prescience, the fish parted before the drifting boat and stayed just out of casting range. Double hauling my chironomidae imitation into the gloaming, I repeatedly came up empty. We sat tight for a little while, hoping they might move closer. With no running lights, though, we wanted to make it back to the resort by dark. Frustrated, we went off in search of Ken. Ken fared better it turned out, taking a pair of 14-inch fish by exploring with a Muddler. I crawled under the bow deck with my beer to get out of the icy air as Steve opened the throttle on the ten-horse Evinrude. It was a gorgeous painter's sunset that evening, ice-blue, pinks, and violets against God's own picket fence.

Only one of several major tributaries that empty into Ross, the Big Beaver Valley stands apart in its importance to anglers and outdoorsmen alike. Aside from being the only tributary open to fishing, the Big Beaver Valley is an arterial into the vast and remote North Cascades wilderness. When Seattle City Light wanted to raise the level of Ross Lake and inundate the lower six miles of valley, a 15-year battle by environmentalists and conservationists ensued. The plans were shelved permanently in 1983. Designated a Research Natural Area, or RNA, an extremely rich and diverse plant community flourishes in the valley —an amazing *20 percent* of the entire number of species found in the North Cascades can be found here. The upper valley is part of the North Cascades grizzly bear ecosystem. A small population of wolves has been sighted in the upper valley. Amphibians and birds thrive in the moist seclusion of the marsh and riverbanks. Trout inhabit the many beaver ponds, and the stream that pulses the life blood of the valley hosts visiting rainbows swimming in to feed after the spring spawn. The U.S. Forest Service packed cutthroat into the Beaver Valley on horseback in 1916, and they have flourished in the beaver ponds.

Early the next morning we were up to Steve's espressos and pancakes. Tom was coming by with the boat to pick us up. We had all our gear strewn on the deck in the morning sun, sipping coffee and dinking with the boats. We'd been told they collapsed into a pack-like unit for hiking, but the biggest challenge was to try to figure how everything we would need for the hike, the pond, our lunch, and the float back down would store in the pockets.

The boat ride up the lake—my God—whump, whump, whump, then up to plane and a roostertail 12-feet high! Valleys and peaks streaming by in and out of fog and clouds and all of us wondering. *Now what's up that valley?* or *What about over that ridge?* Looking at the topo at home I had counted *27* little ponds throughout the valley's short 10-mile length. Apparently there were fish in most of them. But when I asked Tom about this, he said it was really rough going over boggy ground around the ponds and so far he had fished only the one where we were heading. You had to watch out for beaver holes, he warned us, that would drop you like a stone.

Finally we reached the outflow of Beaver Creek, tumbling wildly through the narrow valley entrance into the still waters of the lake. I thought, *We're floating that?* But as we got closer to the galloping water, we notice that it was not just bubbles roiling the surface. There were fish feeding everywhere! We peered into the seams along the current's brisk green edges and glimpsed the flash of mottled backs. We could not fish here, though, for the creek mouths are closed to fishing. *The omen though,* I was thinking, *is good. Very good.*

A short way into the forest we discovered a miniature green Golden Gate-like bridge. Looking down from the center span, the creek looked pretty hairy. "This is the falls," Tom pointed out, "that keeps the bows out of the creek most of the year. We're not floating this part, though, our take-out's a ways upstream."

Canadian dogwood, salal, and swordtail ferns bordered the path leading through groves of ancient red cedar. The effect was sobering. The trail is nicely kept and winds along a primordial forest floor. I felt as if we were going back in time. An hour later we hung a left, bushwhacked a short distance and came out on a gravel bar along a tea-colored creek, the water low in its fall banks.

Looking downstream I saw the water gather and riffle mysteriously out of sight. The water looked delicate and curious. *To heck with the ponds,* I thought. *Let's float.* We wadered up and, carrying our packs over our heads, we forded the creek and scrambled up a steep bluff on the opposite bank. After some dense bushwhacking, we broke out under a wide cerulean sky. The marsh filling the valley floor ahead was a sea of tan grasses. We could see the pond, a glassy body of water—tucked up against a rock massif at the foot of Sourdough Mountain. It was like an eye, set in the earth. Reeds and sedges ringed it like lashes.

Gathering the blackness of the cliff—*it was ebony.* Hiking closer we picked up the icy mountains to the north—*it was topaz.* Once on the water, I could hardly pay attention to fishing. Luna Peak and its pocket glacier drew my eyes north to the vast wilderness of the Pickett Range. *I've floated many a body of water before,* I thought, *but never anything with the sheer poetry of this!*

Kicking along a glassy surface, we trolled Wooly Buggers and streamers, never finding a specific hatch. Hoping to find fish along the shallow edges of the pond, I finned across the lake and fired a marabou leech along the edges and into openings in the reeds—splish, splish, splish. While I came up empty, as did Ken and Steve, it didn't take long for Tom to connect. Again and again, in fact, before any of us touched a trout. Tom's Carey Special was the hot pattern, fished at the end of a 20-foot sink-tip. When we put on sinking lines and tied on the closest thing

Photo by Steve Thomsen

Packing inflated kick boats into the beaver ponds, Luna Peak in distance.
Reminds me of the old Rainier beer commercial.

Photo by Author on Fujifilm

Ken, working the Beaver, fins still on.

Hooked up, finally.

A gorgeous Beaver Creek Cutthroat.

we had to the little streamer, our luck improved considerably. Even with the trout coming along just often enough to encourage anticipation, it was nearly enough to fin leisurely in circles in the heady mountain air.

The fish we picked up that day were all fat, healthy, brightly colored cutts of 12 to 17 inches. Typical of beaver ponds in the Northwest, Johnston told me, the ponds in Beaver Valley hosted an inverterbrate smorgasbord: mayflies, caddis, dragons, damsels, chironomidae, leeches, etc. *I'd like to be here to extract these trout from the reeds come the damsel emergence,* I thought. The occasional slap of a beaver's tail brought our soaring spirits around. We paddled ashore for lunch and ate on the grassy bank.

Looking out on the water, I realized I had detected no rhyme to the location of these fish. Most of them came fairly deep and we had found fish in every quadrant of the lake. A labyrinth of submarine channels, Tom told us, connect the pond complex to the creek. I walked over to inspect a small, shallow body of water connected to the main pond but could see no sign of fish. We fished well into the afternoon, taking more fish by switching to a Carey Special and pulling them deeper. Along about two we paddled ashore, hoisted our boats on our backs and headed back to the creek.

Rainbows in Beaver creek are not always a given. They have a number of obstacles to overcome if they are to make it into the creek at all: an impassable falls at low lake levels, the annual draw-down of the lake in the fall and the heavy glacial flour washing down the Beaver in spring and summer. A week or two in August is typically the only window they have. Some years they are shut out entirely. Johnston estimated only a couple of hundred rainbows were in the Beaver system in any given season, but predicted that more, maybe up to 500, might come along with the boom in lake populations.

After some disastrous years in the late 80s, the population of rainbow in Ross Reservoir has steadily improved. Sexually mature at 13 inches, the size limit for a harvest fishery in the lake was set at just that length. Zooplankton is the primary food source in the lake, and the younger bows, at least, are well adapted to feeding on it. Their gill rakers are closer together than those of the adult fish, enabling them to better harvest this micro-food. The adult trout focus on the insect drift off the stream mouths, and, when conditions permit, swim upstream to forage.

Not only a staging area for pre-spawning fish, but post-spawners as well, streams and stream mouths have always been closed to fishing in the Ross area. Otherwise, the mortality rate for hooking and releasing these recovering fish would be uncomfortably high. By the time they make it upstream in the Beaver, however, the bows will be in pretty good shape. The opening of Big Beaver Creek will be closely monitored to help assess the future of other Ross Lake tributaries. If over use becomes a problem, entry will be subject to available permit. Johnston was excited, though, about the potential: "What you see is the beginning of recognition, I think, by everybody, everywhere, of the value of catch-and-release, non-kill, non-harvest fishery for probably the largest mature, resident, rainbow stock left in the state of Washington," he said. "I don't think there's much question of that. And that it's only going to be getting better."

It was late afternoon when we finally got onstream. A riot of fall golds, reds, and yellows lined the banks—willows, vine maples and red columbines in their autumn finest. Drifting like kelts, we swung under the umbra of giant hillhair one moment and into gulping views of jag-white peaks the next. To top that, mayflies (grey drakes mostly) the size of strawberries were coming off in patches around every bend. Best of all, were the pods of hungry rainbows working them.

The four of us were a few too many for the little creek. Traveling single-file, we would come across a group of feeding fish and try to pull ashore to get out and work them. Nearly all our presentations were downstream and dry, nothing classic about them; any kind of an angle would have been infinitely preferred. Slack lining our casts directly down current and feeding line into the drift was tedious technique, but, my *God,* it was worth it!

We hooked and released both rainbows and cutts in the creek averaging 14 to 15 inches. The rainbows were in fine form, having had a chance to recover from spawning and put on a little weight for winter. I was fishing a little three weight and had my tip in the water much of the time.

The river would swing left, right, riffle quickly, then curve against a tall clay bank. Or it would run like an arrow for 50 yards. The Beaver was the color of black tea in its deeper runs. It was in those pools, where we couldn't see bottom at all, that one of us might lower a nymph.

Ken demonstrated the strike-indicator technique he uses to perfection at one dark bend. Tossing out his fly, he proceeded to feed line into a seemingly unreachable drift. As the bug reached into the curve, we watched the quick disappearance of the white yarn indicator. Wham! Out of one exceptionally difficult curve of water, we watched him extract several scrappy rainbow.

Tom has fished the entire Ross area for quite a while. Friends with one of the biologists here, he helps out with creel samples at the various creeks. He takes most of his fish on nymphs, he told us, "largish Hare's Ears mostly, in natural and olive." This particular day, with its intense surface action, was a surprise.

Fish came up readily to all of our mayfly imitations, even our caddis. We were four excited fly fishermen caravanning down a thumping one-lane stream in a gorgeous wilderness valley. The creek twisted against clay banks and riffled over gravel bottoms. Old, half-buried logs created drop-offs resembling tiny mill dams. The water ran like an epic poem, strident one moment, melodic the next. Sand bars with locals' own footprints (the four-legged variety) bordered the creek from time to time, but more often than not the banks were vertical overhung walls topped with impenetrable foliage. There was no getting in or out of the stream, but, at the one or two places, the trail swung close. Even then, bushwhacking with a boat, like at our put-in and take-out, was nearly comical. Then there were the portages Tom mentioned on the phone. That's portage as in *through* . . . not *around*.

Every so often we came to what appeared to be the end of the line. Barricading the stream from shore to shore would be a massive jumbilation of logs that we would have to try to negotiate. Getting out of our boats while still afloat, dealing with fins and stepping over logs that were partly afloat, then trying to herk our boats along behind without falling in or snagging the tube on a spike branch—then performing an aerial re-entry in ten feet of water—was more than a little challenging.

Well on towards dusk we came around a bend and confronted the mother of all log jams. *Shit,* I thought, *not again.* Thick logs filled the river bed like a cedar dam. We were moaning aloud at the thought of having to negotiate it, when Tom put us at ease by explaining that our take-out was just this side.

We had hooked dozens of fish our first day down the creek. Steve broke his rod on one fish and Tom graciously loaned him his own, then trailed along behind our tiny flotilla, joking and sharing our ebulient spirits. The fishing was so good and so predictable that day that we assumed the cultured ceremony that comes to fly fishermen under the best of conditions.

Photo by Ken Morrish

Tom Barnett on the pond, Luna Peak, again, behind. Tom knows these ponds and the creek better than any man alive.

"After you." "No, no, after you," became the repartee as we took turns casting to each fresh pod.

Back at the resort we were beaming constantly. I couldn't remember the last time I felt so *thoroughly* satisfied. We shot some hoop behind the office to unwind and invited Tom down to join us that night for drinks and a pipe as we edited slides that Steve and Ken had taken a month earlier for another project, a Deschutes summer steelhead story. With a touch of irony, Tom brought down some frozen, farm-raised trout a guest had brought out with him from Idaho, and we ate 'em for dinner.

The next morning we were up early to try to squeeze in another float. Tom drove us up again, but left us on our own this time; we had to move right along to make the rendezvous with him at noon. It was earlier than our float of the previous day, the air cooler. Maybe that accounted for our luck. We didn't see a single bug for the first hour, and, when we finally did, there were no fish working them. In the end, using nymphs, we made only the occasional catch. After an unforgettable day of big drys we were left flatter than a road kill rabbit.

The Big Beaver Valley is refreshing country, whether you're hiking through on your way into the alpine, from which the creek draws its cold, pure waters, or going in to fish. It would be less than responsible of me, though, to sketch a fishery here that was easily accessible. Just getting to the trailhead at the bottom of the little valley is daunting. If you choose to pass on the water taxi or a motorboat rental from the resort, you'll have a nearly prohibitive amount of equipment to pack in and out. And as I said before, floating the creek is difficult, dangerous, and *not* recommended in a conventional float tube.

Jim Johnston probably knows this valley and its fisheries better than anyone else. His last words to me might as well have been his first: *The only last thing is . . this is an area that will not stand much use.* Thinking back on this it occurred to me that a visit to the valley is intrinsically self-limiting, or ought to be, if you know what you're in for; floating Big Beaver Creek is hard work.

To reach the lake and the resort:

Turn off I-5 at Burlington and drive east on Highway #20 for 65 miles to Diablo. If you're coming from the east, from Winthrop, drive west on Highway 20 for 68 miles. Once at Diablo, cross the dam, turn right and park nearby at the Ross Lake Resort parking lot. A Seattle City Light boat leaves twice daily from the public dock at Diablo. For a $5.00 fare, it will deliver you across Diablo Lake to the base of Ross Dam. The ride is peaceful, scenic and impressive as you enter the narrow canyon at the base of Ruby Mountain. The resort will send down a truck to shuttle you up. They will also shuttle canoes and kayaks for a nominal fee.

If you're planning a canoe or kayak trek of the lake, you can launch at the Colonial Creek boat launch on Diablo Lake, then paddle under the highway bridge to the base of Ross Dam.

For the more energetic, a 6.8-mile trail leads from Diablo to the lake at Ross Lake Resort. Alternately, you can descend from the parking lot along Highway 20 at milepost #134 on a lovely trail through a forest of Douglas fir and lodgepole pine to the level of the lake along the eastern shore. However, you must call over to the resort and have them pick you up in their launch to get to the trail-head on the opposite shore. Call the resort ahead of time and they will give you the location of the phone. The East Bank Trail is accessed from Highway 20, some two miles further east, and will swing you around the deep Ruby Arm.

The resort is open June 18th—October 31st, but Tom is around much of the off season as well. Tom has the complete low down on the Beaver and a fleet of boats to get you where you want to go. Call for a brochure, availability, and rates.

Bikes are banned from all the trails in the Recreation Area, so, unless you're going all the way to B.C. with them in the boat, there's no point in bringing them.

Backcountry permits are required to camp in the area. You can get one at the ranger station in Marblemount or Diablo or, as a last resort, at the ranger's cabin tethered to Ross Dam.

For a complete list of excellent hiking trips out of the lake, pick up101 Hikes in the North Cascades and Trips and Trails, published by The Mountaineers—detailed information, helpful maps and a list of topos specific for each trip originating from the lake. The Mountaineers Clubhouse Bookstore, 300 Third Avenue West, Seattle, Washington 98119, (206) 284-8484 carries both, as do many other bookstores.

For Resort or Water Taxi information, contact Tom Barnett at Ross Lake Resort, Rockport, WA 98283 (206) 386-4437.

For back country information, contact the Ranger Station at Marblemount: (206) 873-4590

The Yakima

Photo by Author on Fujifilm

Apples, sagebrush, sunshine . . .
and plenty of rainbows.

Believe me, my young friend, there is
nothing—absolutely nothing—*half so*
much worth doing as simply messing
about in boats.

Mole to Water Rat, *Wind in the Willows*
- Kenneth Grahame

Appeared originally in *Fly Rod & Reel*

It was a fine mid-summer night in Washington's central desert, the night wind warm still, blowing through the ring of willows surrounding Murphy's. It was well after midnight, too, and we were late arriving at the country B&B popular with visiting fly fishermen. My wife Pamela and I stood sheepishly outside a screened rear verandah. Windows rattled as I opened the sealed door, stepped to the rear of the dark house, and knocked three times. Interminable minutes later we could hear footsteps in the bowels of the old building. Suddenly, we were awash in light; a woman in a dark robe stood in the open door. That would be Doris Callahan, who had kindly gotten out of bed to let in her wayward guests. We fell asleep that night with our windows open, while outside we could hear the rustle of willow boughs and the hiss of all-night sprinklers.

Awake early the next morning to the aroma of fresh-baked pastry wafting through the century-old farmhouse, Pamela went down to investigate. She returned a few minutes later with a funny look on her pretty face.

"You won't believe it," she said. "There is bakery stuff on *every* available surface—pastries, coffee-cakes, pies, muffins, turnovers, and some delicious-looking units I've never seen before. At first I thought it was all for us, you know, like it was some kind of test or something."

We had a good laugh at this, then hurried down to get scored. Doris, as it turns out, is not only an inn-keeper, but a first-class baker. The pastries were for local restaurants in Ellensburg. After a large, delicious breakfast, we met up with our guide, Nick Pallis, in the parking lot of a local convenience store.

My first impression was of a well-strung mind in a large, loosely-strung body. Easy going and quick to smile, Nick had a soft voice and an open ear. He was also, as we soon discovered, precise, articulate, and about as knowledgeable a guy as there is on the Yakima River. He checked over our gear while Pamela ran into the store to get a loaf of bread and some ice. "The Yakima's running high," he told me. Not much later we parked our rig under stately cottonwoods and stepped out beside a river. *No kidding,* I thought.

At about 4300 cfs, there was dear little definition to a sheet of green water barreling south. Still, it was a gorgeous color, with a light, jade-green cast. The Yakima is a fertile river. In fact, the growth rate is quite high and the trout average nearly a foot. It is a large wild trout population of predominantly rainbow with some cutthroat and a small number of browns.

The watershed is large. Drawing from deep in the Cascade mountains, the fertile upper and middle Yakima Valley was called "Too Virgin," or "Big Belly," by the native tribes. This stumped me at first until someone pointed out that "Big Belly" might refer to a nutrional condition, not a feminine one. In earlier times the river was a conduit of dependable salmon runs. These, combined with edible Camas roots, berries, elk, and grouse might have made the natives big bellied, indeed. The river descends from its headwaters near Snoqualmie Pass, down through groves of lodgepole pine, into rolling hills of sagebrush where the river bank supports a narrow riparian zone and a belt of scattered cottonwood and white alder. Farmers, drawing from the life blood of the valley, nourish crops of apples, mint and hops where once there was only desert.

Midsummer in the Yakima Valley is irrigation time. Washington's premier apple groves thrive in this once-barren land. From three upriver dams comes a powerful flush of cold water. With the resultant high flow, there is little subtlety to the river's sinuous course, little definition to a river that in both spring and fall reveals a svelte form.

I waded out a bit to have a look up and downstream. Although

Photo by Author on Fujifilm

Pamela, on the rocks.

Photo by Steve Thomsen

One of the larger rainbow we caught that day.

Photo by Author on Fujifilm

The Yakima River Canyon, downriver from Ellensburg.

Photo by Pamela Maresten

Nick and the author perusing fly options.

I could make out some semblance of pocket, eddy, and shallows; it was all about as delicate as a speeding truck. There was one spot, though, just across from the launch. On impulse I had brought along my own kick-boat, thinking I could run it with fins and anchor up when I wanted. I set it up, strung up a rod, fussed with what to bring along, then rowed across.

I waded up a tapering riffle, fishing it eagerly to the head. When I laid a large, black woolly worm near the top, it was immediately grabbed. A bright, sky-borne rainbow auspiciously inaugurated the day.

A couple of fish later, we pulled into midstream and drifted with the current. After floating only a couple of miles, two things became evident. Not only was there too much flow to use the fins effectively, there was too much current for my little ten-pound anchor. The first time I dropped it and came up tight I was a little anxious at how violently my pontoons deflected in the hard flow. Then, when I went to weigh it, I couldn't get it unstuck. Pulling hard on the rope threatened to flip me over. The water pressure against the pontoons was enormous. I was relieved when Nick finally floated down behind and pulled it free. I stashed my boat in a clump of sagebrush along the bank and made a threesome in Nick's handsome dory. Leaning into the stern thigh-brace and working out some line, I reflected back on a few headstrong clients of my own when I was a guide. I called out an earnest "thanks" over my shoulder for Nick's patience with my separate agenda.

Nick directed my attention to overhanging sedges and grasses, around hummocks and stick-ups and the shallower flanks running over an aerated bottom of cobble/pebble/small boulder. He suspected we were drifting at about three to four miles an hour; to me it seemed more like six or seven. The gradient was low; there were no rapids to speak of on the entire river. It was mostly the lack of definition that rendered the impression of speed, the continuous sweep of water without pools and few riffles to punctuate the drift. In any case, I was more used to fishing on my feet than out of a chariot.

We could have done much worse, however, than winging dries on the fly. The scent of the sagebrush and mineral-rich water filled our heads; the snowy green Yakima was a tonic to the eyes. After spending a day on (and under, when we flipped) the Methow (another desert river, but this one running an ugly chocolate brown and just below flood stage), I was happy to be drifting the Yakima. The greenish cast is largely suspended matter, a stew of minerals, algae and phytoplankton. The insects are abundant, especially mayfly, caddis and stone. Anyone used to crystal-clear waters might find these large-scale, freestone-style rivers rather mysterious; it has always been so for me. Getting to know the prolific bug life on the Deschutes in the early 80s was exciting enough at one point to get Rick Haefle on the phone and grill him about how many of my English Lit credits he thought might apply to a major in Aquatic Biology.

While the Yakima is certainly fertile, it can be a tactical puzzle. Virtually a tail-water fishery, its biological cycles are impacted by flow cycles. Irrigation of the apple groves requires a steady flush of water from upstream dams from about mid-July through October. Come fall, with the release of salmon smolts and a reduced need for agrarian demands, the flow is reduced to about 1800 cfs, prime conditions for wading fishermen.

Nick spoke a little of the complexity: "We'll be fishing almost primarily from the boat during the mid-summer months, whereas in the spring and fall, especially the fall, we're able to get out and do a lot more wading. Before that, it's primarily a boat fishery, or best approached from the banks. The cold water is too deep and too fast for wading in most places.

"I've seen the river as low as 275 cfs in the fall, and we've fished it as high as 6500 cfs in the spring, which is just cranking. What'll happen is they'll have it right around 1500, 2500 in late spring—April, May—and then they'll start to crank the flows up come mid-June for irrigation purposes. It'll average anywhere between 2500 and 4000 throughout the midsummer months, then they'll start to taper it down. Then, once they get right around September 10th, 12th, 14th, right in there, they'll just shut it right down. It'll go from 3500 right down to 1250, 750, and then 500, just within about a three-day, four-day shot. That puts the fish off for a few days anyway. They'll pod up though, definitely, and once those Baetis start coming off . . . wow!"

High summer mornings in flowering deserts along green, trout-filled rivers are tops in my book; the Yakima that morning was another chapter. It was a weekday, and we had the river nearly to ourselves. Two eagles and one osprey soared high over the drifting boat. The sun was a torch, but the air cool with a fresh breeze over the water. Tiny eddies swirled along the rip-rap where black trout emerged from submarine crevices, darting after emerging bugs floating off the bottom, or slashing into tiny adults dawdling at the surface. And the river was always pressing, urging us along.

It was stimulating, high-speed fishing that day on the Yakima. Reading the lies ahead in large print, by direction of flow and available cover—all the while cast, mend, drift, lift, false cast and cast again . . . and *strike!*—it was highly visceral fishing, more an athletic experience than a tactical one . . . my favorite kind.

Nick and I involuntarily set up a chorus of "ooooo's" and "aaahhh's" watching the fly cruise through the *creme de la creme*. So *much* of it looked good though, so much of the water tight along the bank was just Trout Club Med. We got so caught up in this, that Pamela laughed.

"It's a good thing I've got my eye on you two," she said, grinning. "You sound like a couple of love birds." But firing the little dries in tight under the bank where the little ersastz bugs twirled and drifted was just too much to keep quiet about. We stopped for lunch on a gravel bar mid-river just after noon and gave the adrenals a rest.

Primarily a rainbow fishery, trout populations on the Yakima have never been decimated as they have on other popular rivers. According to historical creel counts, even during the "Catch and Kill" days there were decent numbers of fish around. After the special regs went into place in the early 80s, both the fishing and the fish noticeably improved. Within recent years a "Catch and Release" policy has gone into effect throughout most of the river. Now the Yakima is arguably the best wild trout fishery in the state. You can even fish it year round now, upriver from Roza dam. Over the horizon of this success, drift a vagrant cloud or two. Storm cloud or not, no one knows for sure.

In recent years there has been quite a bit of controversy over a plan to return anadromous fish to their ancestral drainages. A year ago last March the word was final—a pair of hatcheries will soon be under construction for the Yakima. The first of these, located in Cle Elum, will raise a quarter of a million baby Chinook for release. Both coho and Chinook will be raised. Steelhead will be considered as time and funds permit. The Yakima Alliance is a group concerned with possible side effects of the Yakima/Klickitat Production Project, as the hatchery project is called. Their primary concern is that a good thing might get worse. No one can say with certainty whether resident trout will be displaced by foraging salmon smolts, or whether the fragile native steelhead stocks may be negatively impacted by hatchery fish. Baseline studies are under way to establish existing trout fishery data to be effectively monitored after the introduction of anadro-

Photo by Author on Fujifilm

Pamela, working a downstream nymph.

Photo by Richard Ward

Author, working a seam.

mous fish. The project will use a progressive "Adaptive Management Policy," which, while it *is* a plan based on action versus non-action, allows, at least, for the assimilation of new data and change—even to the point of project termination.

We anchored up from time to time, usually in thigh-deep water flushing over broken bottom. Overhung banks left the shallows in a thin crust of shade. With the cooler high water that day, fish were hanging there and working spotty hatches of pale morning duns and slightly larger caddis. We took fish from each stop, healthy looking rainbows, but only of small to moderate size. I was hoping to tie into one of the bigger trout I had heard about.

A little Matthews X-Caddis or an Elk Hair would elicit a splashy take as often as not. I had a full box of hoppers with me, but it was a little early still for the spring-leggeds. The bigger rainbows would be out picking off a more substantial meal of nymph or larvae. We had an eye out for signs of one of these, though, hoping one might be parked in a particularly productive lie with his head up. It was such wonderfully kinesthetic dry fly fishing that I did not want to bother with a nymph simply to catch bigger fish. As I worked the shore like a one-man band, Nick talked about hatches on the Yakima.

"Hmm, let's see," he said, taking a lick on his oar. "You've got a fairly strong stonefly hatch that comes off in the spring—April or May. Not nearly as prolific as, say, that of the Deschutes or the Madison. A really decent caddis fly hatch that comes off right around Mother's Day and will stay strong, very strong, for a good couple months, and, in fact, throughout the whole summer, really, petering off toward the end of August, beginning of September.

"The pale morning duns will come off starting right about mid-May and will really peak by about the middle of June and then will start to wane, and by mid-July they're pretty much done. There are some green drakes out in the spring as well. March and April and into May there's a fairly decent March brown hatch. In fact, this last year was one of the better years I've seen for the March browns. They've been kind of weak over the last two or three years.

"There are some good yellow sallies throughout the summer months—June, July, and August—then, let's see, hopper fishing will really start to come on by the first of August—in fact it's just now starting to come on. And that's pretty strong for a good month. Then, once September rolls around, of course, the Baetis start coming on. *Really* decent Baetis hatches throughout September, October and November. In fact, throughout the winter. Then, during the winter months and on into spring, we have good midge activity."

Access to the popular stretch of river between Cle Elum and Ellensburg is very good. The highway that parallels much of the Yakima is a two-lane, scenic drive that affords nearly unrestricted access throughout most of the river's lower length. Highway 126, I was reading in the paper the other day, especially as it winds up through the Yakima River Canyon, happens to hold the state's top honors for vehicular casualties. Coming off the river in a state of blind bliss, it is mostly drunken rafters that become statistics. The few places where the river leaves the road in the Canyon, you can pull over most anywhere you want and fish the rip-rap, or a tight-looking grass bank, or a log jam that you know must be a hangout for the alpha trout in that particular stretch. Or you can cross over one of the foot bridges to access the opposite shore and hike the railroad tracks, stopping to scramble down to fish the bank.

For those who want to get away from the road, there is the

upper Yakima from, say, Cle Elum to Thorpe, where you can hike into relatively quiet stretches of water. There is quite a bit of private property along through here, but most homeowners don't mind a fisherman along the river. There is some excellent water through this stretch and the aesthetic factor is high.

The big fella was tucked in with his flank to the reeds. It was nearly dusk.

Nick's sharp eye had noticed its back breaking water a moment before. In a flash, the anchor was released and the boat brought up short; I grabbed hold of the rail to keep from falling over. A moment later we all caught sight of the leisurely breach of one machismo trout.

Hard to get a fly to, though; the fish was tucked back in among the reeds. There was no hatch, and it appeared to be feeding opportunistically on the occasional meal washing by.

"Tough lie," Nick announced.

No doubt it would be difficult to get a drag-free drift into this boy. There were overhanging reeds immediately upriver, and the quick water inches from his lie would suck the slack out of my drift like a vacuum cleaner. I had on a #14 Stimulator at this point and tightened my loop to a mere few inches. I would try to overpower a lateral cast to get some built-in mend. I pushed it in hard against the reeds. It worked slick and swung the fly around downstream of the line . . . but no takers.

After a good 20 minutes of working over this fish, I gave the rod to Nick. Ten minutes later we had some luck. As the big fish came up to take our fly, Nick struck home and the fish careened downriver. We had seen enough to know it was a large bow, but the deep angle to the line was surprising. We decided to work as a team to land it, and, while I fought the big trout around and under the boat, Nick readied the net, Pamela the camera.

It fought like a good channel cat, running deep and strong. No aerial stuff, but a dogged, surging fight with deep directional changes; we never saw it till the end. Pamela snapped a couple photos of it in the net and released it to the river. We congratulated each other on this, our joint finale operation, and quietly drifted the last quarter mile in fading light to the takeout.

It had been a refreshing, vigorous day of fishing. I'd been point rod for six hours (with a very sore right arm) as Nick gracefully swept us from one side of the river to the other, knowing the river like his own kitchen, setting up hair-perfect each time. The warm mahogany hues of Nick's dory were a fine aesthetic contrast with the cold ribbon of water sweeping us south. The three of us floating along the Yakima had something of the excitement and the sociability of the Water Rat and the Mole on their own fine river morning. It had been some enjoyable trout fishing indeed, and, not in the least, a fine time messing about in boats.

Yakima

Where To Stay:
Hotels or motels in either Ellensburg or Cle Ellum will do the trick. If you want more of the homey flavor of this world-renown apple valley, the bed and breakfasts will speak better to that— Murphy's was excellent. For those who enjoy a continuous communion with the places fishing takes us, there are a number of campgrounds, both public and private, to choose from.

How to get there:

At about 100 miles from Seattle, Interstate 90 will deliver you over the Snoqualmie Mountains to the headwaters of the Yakima and down into the Yakima Valley. Highway 97 will lead you along the upper river, and Highway 821 follows the river through the Yakima Canyon.

Books, Maps:

Recreational Users Map of the Yakima River
Kittitas County Field & Stream Club
P.O. Box 522
Ellensburg, WA 98926
Fax: (509) 964-2413 (no phone)

The River Journal: Yakima River
Frank Amato Publications
P.O. Box 82112
Portland, OR 97282
503-653-8108

B&Bs:

Murphy's Country B&B
Doris Callahan, proprietor
2830 Thorpe Highway South
Ellensburg, WA 98926
(509) 925-7986

Private Campgrounds:

KOA
Ellensburg, WA
West Interchange I-90
(509) 996-2258

Guides and Tackle:

Angler's Fly Fishing Guide Service
Nick Pallis
P.O. Box 828
Mercer Island, WA 98040
(425) 643-4741

Kaufmann's Streamborn
1-800-442-4359

Fishermen Who Paddle
With the Whales

Photo by Author on Fujifilm

*Do you reckon Tom Sawyer would ever
go by this thing? Not for pie he wouldn't.
He'd call it an adventure—that's what
he'd call it; and he'd land on that wreck
if it was his last act.*

Huck Finn, *Adventures of Huckleberry Finn*
- Mark Twain

Appeared originally in *Fly Rod & Reel*
titled, "Voyage of the Sea Lyon"

The Inside

I was nearly two weeks underway at this point, paddling north along Vancouver Island's protected eastern shore and looking for a spot of beach to camp for the night when I noticed something fussin' in the water ahead. I got out the glasses and was excited to discover that the commotion was caused by salmon, not seals as I had suspected. From the nautical chart strapped to the center console of my kayak I could see that I was approaching the mouth of the Oyster River.

Paddling closer, I discovered several large schools of salmon milling just out of reach of the handful of fishermen standing on shore. I spent the next hour excitedly chasing salmon around, alternately trolling and casting a fly to bright, six-pound fish. It was an exercise in frustration as I finally gave up and paddled onto the beach not far from the river mouth. Leaning back against a huge driftwood log, a burly guy with a pony tail greeted me warmly.

This would be Rory Glennie, who, along with the rest of his family, and as many fly rods, were waiting for the salmon to move closer to shore, as they did, he told me, each evening. Ironically, Rory was the recent president of the local chapter of the B.C. Steelhead Society. *Not bad timing for a fly fishing journalist*, I thought, and while we waited for the salmon, Rory filled me in on the local scene. From seal predation on the Puntledge, to improving salmon runs on the Strait-side streams, there seemed to be both a lot under way, and yet a lot left to do. As we talked, I noticed two scruffy-looking men hiking up the beach toward us in the distance. They would stop every once in a while to toss out a treble hook with a weight attached and jerk it back to shore. Apparently Rory was not only outspoken on the podium; when the snaggers stopped in front of us to cast, I was sure they heard

Rory's remark about "the low-life on the beach these days." I thought for sure we'd be in for a fuss, but they never turned around.

I watched Rory hook four or five salmon that evening but came up empty myself. He gave me the hot fly, a little epoxy minnow imitiation painted a pink hue, but the best I could manage was a bump. With the sun down, the air took on a chill and Rory had waded wet. We all sat together around a crackling fire drinking beer, warming up, and talking. He told me the story of the pinks and how you needed to get the attention of a group of fish to get a strike instead of fishing to just one, and suggested it might be a competitive reflex. Later on, when everyone had left, I had the beach and, it seemed, the universe, to myself.

I was grateful for Rory and his family; somehow their pleasant reception on the beach that afternoon seemed like a welcome, somehow, into my long journey as well. The moon rose full and flooded the sea with a twinkling ivory light that night, and I lay in my bag under the stars feeling really good and listening to the lapping of waves. I could sense how I was coming in relation to the moon and sun now, instead of watches and calenders. I had left home on a crescent; now it was full. By the time I reached the tip of the island it would probably be new again. When the sun heated up my tent, I got up; when I couldn't see anymore, I went to bed. *To hell with calendars,* I thought, *I like this supernal reckoning.*

It looked to be an exciting summer; paddling a kayak alone around the perimeter of Vancouver Island would make sure of that. As for the fishing, I knew only that I would encounter streams and rivers with fish schooling off the mouths, primarily on the inside, and on the outside, a *tabula rasa* of fishing opportunities. Therein lay the deepest beauty of it all for me. I would find fish where I found them. Salmon, ling, bass. I would catch them and eat them to keep my body strong. If they were too big for one person, I would let them go, and sometimes, when I was in the thick of a school, I would catch three or four, or five or six even, and be sated, and put the rod back in its holder and pick up the paddle. It was raw stuff, though. Once I passed Campbell River it was a blank canvas . . . no lengendary waters or hallowed streams, only a remote and fertile sea where very few people had ever wet a fly

My friends thought it was *quite* the undertaking, maybe a bit too much to chew, but I figured differently. I had everything a guy might need to undertake a trip like this—equipment, experience, good information, all the charts and tables—I had it all. More importantly, I had drive. Like *shit happens*—well, *people do stuff*—It seemed as simple as that. I was aiming for deserted, sun-drenched beaches at the edge of a thumping North Pacific Ocean and a mother-lode of wilderness fly fishing potential. I knew it would be a stretch from time to time, but I was ready and I was jazzed. As for solo, paddling alone through this marine paradise would be nourishing for the soul. It was enough to have my own busy mind on the scene; I didn't need another.

Ivan Doig's *Sea Runners* gives a rugged account of several men in a dugout canoe travelling down the northwest coast; I read that before I left. A friend of mine, Craig Petersen, paddled around with another guy in kayaks four years ago; his insight, along with a copy of his route with notations penciled on a chart of Vancouver Island, was invaluable.

I had accumulated a dozen charts of my own, one for each section of the coast, and there were tide tables and current charts for the straits and channels. I had Ince and Kotner's *A Paddler's Guide to the West Coast* and Washburne's *A Coastal Kayaker's Manual* with me for referance.

I had the *safest* (open-cockpit), *strongest* (kevlar), *largest* (technically a double) kayak possible for such a trip. It was built with a molded seat on top of an airtight hull; should I capsize, I could simply flip the boat over and hop back on. I wore a wet suit and had a life-jacket always close at hand. I had a two-way radio to send out a Mayday, and I had flares. My days as a river guide, planning ahead for every eventuality during five days of rowing through a roadless canyon, would pay dividends.

Frankly, I was petrified at the thought of getting trapped off-shore alone in building seas. On the other hand, it was an in-tensely vibrant and compelling place to be; I knew that some of my fears were not entirely rational and would haunt me the rest of my life if I turned my back on them. My biggest job on this adventure was to trust in myself, in my plan, and in my equip-ment. Paddling alone for a prolonged period meant carrying a big load. Fortunately, the boat, a Tsunami X-2 Starship (is that a name or what?), was more freighter canoe than sporty kayak. I stuffed it to the gills and had Pamela mail out 40-pound packages of supplies to post offices at Campbell River, Port Hardy and Tofino.

Although it took to within two weeks of my departure date on July 11th to get my boat, the Sea Lyon, up to the islands, I was busy soliciting the rest of my gear and trying to raise enough money to check out of my life for what I expected to be a couple of months. In the end, I managed to come up with everything necessary to make the trip and just enough money to shoestring a budget of sorts. I had everything spread out on a beach on Lopez Island one windy afternoon in early July, fielding questions and good-byes from friends and local news folks. An hour later I was gone.

As I paddled north toward Cape Scott I found more and more fly fishermen wading off the mouths of rivers like the Nimpkish, the Cluxewe, and, the Keogh. It was rumored to be a big year for

Entering the Canadian Gulf Islands. Beautiful paddling locale, although lacking the excitement of the outer coast.

Photo by Author on Fujifilm

Author with fresh salmon. Such self-timed shots were extremely challenging, I had to carry the fish over, trip the shutter, and scurry back into position—sometimes forgetting where that was exactly.

Photo by Author on Fujifilm

pinks, and, from the amount of fish I found milling off stream mouths or steaming around in big spanking schools, I'd have to agree. Paddling north along the eastern shore of Vancouver Island, my mind often soared on ahead. Fifty miles due west lay one of the most remote and unexplored stretches of deserted white-sand beaches on the continent. Fifty miles as the raven flew maybe, but a month more of paddling for me. I had wonderful memories of a particular beach there too . . . *a deserted beach where the wind is hot and scented with the spicy aroma of cedar and filled with the call of loons and ravens and the lapping of waves. Gregg howls at night for the wolves to come out of the mountains to visit, and we all keep one eye out for cougar when we walk the edge of the beach where the forest rises up like a jungle; a friend had been mauled on the island the year before. The exquisite, black-haired Summer Moon is with us, as is Jaime, her exquisite black-haired lover. There are children and elders and a core of eager, long haired bucks. Not your average excursion—it is an annual migration, a month long pilgrimage. We are naked most of the time, and, when we aren't fishing, we are hiking untracked beaches, or playing* pitanque *or carving bowls or masks or rubbing our salty bodies together in tents, or simply getting high at the edge of the world . . . but mostly we are fishing, and extraordinary fishing it is.*

El Niño *delivered the rapacious mackeral close to shore that year. How many times had I mistaken the powerful first run of one of these iridescent bullets for a salmon? There are plentiful schools of coho and a few Chinook . . . we take them trolling from our kayaks, using unweighted flies along the surface. We have a skiff along for support and fish from it, too, and the salmon are so aggressive that we feel the boat shudder now and again as they attack the prop!*

When we find a herring ball, we stop and cast into it. The take is firm; the run immediate. If I am nearby a bed of kelp, they tangle me up; if not, it is hard work keeping up with a fish like the coho that changes directions every few seconds. And if I'm lucky enough to bring it alongside the kayak, there is dear little place to put a flopping ten-pound salmon!

The sun quickly heated up my tent the next morning. I dripped a cup of coffee and tried again for a small pod of salmon near shore, but no dice. Then I bent to it and made the remaining distance to Campbell River that day, spurred on by the knowledge that once past this largish fishing center and mill town I would leave civilization behind. I spoke with Craig Orr by phone before leaving home. Craig was the current president of B.C.'s Steelhead Society and had suggested whom to get in touch with when I made Campbell River.

Dave Hadden is tall and lanky and reminded me of a cowboy logger. He picked me up at the government wharf and drove to the Campbell River Lodge. I was nearly broke and not really wanting to spend the money to sleep in a wooden box anyway when I could lodge at nature's Best Western every night carte blanche. Camping around cities is the worst, however, so when Dave insisted he was paying that night's bill, I did not have my heart in a refusal.

After living out-of-doors for the last few weeks I found my new digs in the lodge nothing short of bizarre. I had a shower, a television, telephone, and neighbors, but I dug it for the change it was. The starched and sterile sheets against my sun-baked body seemed somehow like a metaphor for my whole edge with urbanity. *After all,* I reminded myself, *it is not by accident that I live on an island.*

The cavernous lodge was a balm after the seething asphalt heat of the parking lot outside. Once past the receptionist's window, you entered another world. After wandering down dark, wood-paneled hallways into the bowels of the rambling building, I found the subterranean bar as cool as shaded ice on that 90-degree day and drank up several frosty draft beers. Outside the sliding glass doors of the bar was a patio latticed with colorful Canadian beer-logoed umbrellas. Situated right on the banks of the Campbell, the lodge is the destination point for local guides who row their dories right up to a weigh station on the back lawn where the great Tyee salmon are weighed. Roderick Haig-Brown was a great fan of this past-time and, of course, lived just upstream along the river. Dave picked me up that evening, after I'd had a chance to shower and rustle a quick washing of clothes, and we drove up along the Campbell together to check it out.

Dave told me how hard-hit the native runs of steelhead and salmon were. After talking with Rory and Craig and Dave, I was getting a feel for the degree of environmental awareness and activism of the Canadian fly fisherman. "Somebody's gotta stir the pot," was how Rory put it. Dave told me that, with the logging boom early in this century, the valley bottoms were easiest pickings. Little regard was given the streams and rivers at that time. With no protective legislation in place, timber was harvested right to the banks and resulted in log jams, flooding, and the subsequent silting in of spawning beds and a wholesale decline of the native fishes that once called these waterways home. Moreover, the run of wild steelhead native to the Campbell was exterminated through damming and heavy metal contaminaton from nearby mines. Dave told me there was a ray or two of hope in this storm-cloud picture. A recent emphasis on protecting native stock instead of relying on put-and-take hatchery replacements has developed, and a "catch and release" regulation governing all native steelhead has been implemented island-wide.

It was refreshing to see a man who makes his living in the

Mom and the boys. The black bears on Vancouver were infinitely preferred to the grizzlies of Alaska, where I carried a shotgun.

Relaxing in camp with the first aid kit. I did not pack this chair around the island; I found it on the beach.

Photo by Gregg Blomberg Photography

Sea Otters. These guys were reintroduced on the West coast after their wholesale slaughter in the 19th century, and are a stable population again. Guaranteed to make you smile.

Photo by Author on Fujifilm

First salmon of the trip. One of the student body of an enormous school of fish at the mouth of the Keogh River, near Port Hardy. The device in my hand is called a Bogagrip. It secures and weighs the fish.

logging industry and still has a conscience about the ecosystems integral to everyone's livelihood. I thought, *it is so tempting to justify vocation.* Dave and a couple of other fellows have taken it upon themselves to patrol the Campbell, which above a certain point is "fly fishing only." There are only a couple of game wardens for an enormous amount of territory here, and, without the support of people like Dave, the enforcement of the hard-earned conservation legislation would be nearly impossible. We came upon two young men from California setting up their spinning rods within the fly-fishing-only deadline that evening. Dave firmly, but gently, explained to the men they were on the wrong stretch of river. Dave showed me the signs they had posted along the river and told me he makes a tour every evening after work.

We didn't fish that day but just hiked along and looked out on the water instead. Laying eyes on a fine river like the Campbell was nourishing for me and reminded me in several places of my beloved Deschutes. And after weeks of Mother sea, it felt very grounding to look upon the Campbell. I could sync with this river, its direction and intent, whereas the soul of the sea was like a distant galaxy.

From Campbell River north the seaways tightened, and humanity fell away like a cliff. It was great to put civilization behind and paddle north into increasing wilderness now. Instead of the immense Strait of Georgia, I paddled narrowing straits and channels with ravens calling in the treetops overhead. Currents were different, too; tide-rips and whirlpools were always to be watched for. That portion of the Pacific Ocean that sluices through this neck of the woods is forced through a lacy network of channels. If it weren't for the tides, it wouldn't be much, but, with the push and pull of trillions of gallons of water twice each day, it was as if old Neptune were plunging the works. I got into more than one squirrelly piece of water that boiled up suddenly from deep and active hydraulics.

The fishing fleet was parked along the way awaiting the opening of the pink salmon season; floating cans and bottles were much in evidence. They were a pretty friendly bunch, though. One guy named Sam, who reminded me of a healthy old tree, waved me over and gave me a salmon. A bunch of Norwegian fishermen from Vancouver invited me aboard their boat where I sat down in the galley with the crew to enormous plates of delicious fried fish fillets and a big salad. These were great, hot summer days, and I came across more schools of pinks, jumping and breaching as they milled off river mouths or steaming past rolling their black backs in the glinting sun. Nonetheless, try as I might, I did not pick up my first salmon until just east of Port Hardy.

Coming in sight of the Keogh River, I noticed several schools of salmon, breaking water. The sun was out, and it was a gorgeous day in the north country, especially welcome after a chilly and fog-shrouded morning. I was anxious to reach Port Hardy and my next food drop, but I paddled over to investigate. Alongshore a pair of fly fishermen had waded out to cast. A hundred yards off, in a small outboard, a young man and a woman were trolling. As yet, I hadn't seen anyone hook up. Gradually, however, I became aware of the immensity of the schools of fish.

The water darkened and twinked with silver as they passed beneath my kayak. Everywhere I looked for half a mile there were fish! Before long a Canadian Fisheries boat sped our way, sounding like a bunch of excited kids as they took stock of the returning bonanza. Then the young couple in the boat hooked up, a bright silvery salmon that jumped in the morning sun and inaugurated a marvellous day of fishing.

Chasing the schools around to get within casting range, I

would drop the paddle in my lap and pick my rod out of the Downeast holder bolted just behind my hip I was pretty quick on the draw by the time the trip was over. I fished a seven-foot sink-tip and retrieved in short strips. In the back of my mind I had Rory's advice about swimming the fly past a group of fish; I was so in the thick of it now that I could feel the fly sliding over their backs! Whenever I felt a hesitation I would strike, and there was no way around snagging an occasional fish. Most of the fish were between five and seven pounds and good fighters, taking 40 to 50-yards of line on their initial runs, but they didn't jump like cohos. These were strong fish, though, still very bright, and they would run all around the bay with me in tow. Sometimes they broke me off in the ubiquitous kelp beds as I caught sight of their two-foot bodies twisting in the emerald water in the shadow of the boat. I hooked eight or ten salmon that morning and felt the same kind of welcoming from the fish that I'd recieved from Rory and his family. Finally the ice was broken!

I spent the night sleeping on the government wharf under the gangplank at Port Hardy (definitely the seediest digs of the entire trip). After the bars shut down, I awoke to drunken fishermen trooping down the noisy plank followed by several bereft (and equally drunk) women screaming curses at them at the top of their lungs. I was happy to get underway early the next day. *Humanity . . . bah! Civilization . . . double bah!*

Leaving Port Hardy, I noticed the boat was bulging more than ever before. I had received a huge package in the mail at the Port, inordinately bigger than the others, and I had picked up some extra supplies in town as well. Among the rest of my gear I carried two tents, one a roomy North Face dome for long lay-overs, the other a bivvy sack that came in most useful skulking around marinas and ports, pitching it in the bushes and furtive hobo spots (I used the tents more for protection from mosquito gangs than from rain). I carried a lot of other stuff, including a gas stove, wet suits, clothes, complete camera equipment and a box of micro-cassettes for recording the journey, a sail, water bottles, a water purifying pump, a dozen books and charts, plenty of dehydrated food and a horrendous stash of PowerBars (240, to be exact) and, of course, enough beer to get me to the next outpost. The beer, I was delighted to discover, served as excellent ballast.

I carried 20 lbs of delicious cranberry-cashew granola sent to me by Mike Papet at Just Good Foods. I ate Powerbars for lunch on the water, and feasted on fresh fish, as often as not, for dinner. I had a hand-line along for easy bottom fishing, and I knew my edible sea vegetables, which I ate whenever I came across them. I thought it was pretty cool to be able to reach out and pluck a sprig of floating *fucus* (high in vitamin C) out of the cold saltwater and pop it into my mouth without missing a stroke.

I found a bit of heaven in a little bay harboring a small river and another school of pinks after a long day in the saddle from Port Hardy. I was not alone, however; it was one of the rare beaches I shared with anyone on the trip. I enjoyed the company of Shawn Cotler, a commercial kayak guide who put on a show catching several pinks on a fly from shore at dusk. Broker than a stick, I was happy to help Shawn out with a reel upgrade by trading him my back-up Marryat and spool for some hard Canadian cash.

I came across a pod of grey whales feeding very close to shore within two miles of Cape Scott on the evening of the 15th of August, a little over a month from my launch. It was humbling to be in the presence of these large mammals and a bit disconcerting as they breached ten feet away. I was never sure whether they had me on their radar or not. I camped that night in a little bay beside the milling beasts.

Besides their regular exhalation, whales sometimes make a funny whistling sound, like blowing across the mouth of a bottle. A fog bank drifted in that evening, and I could hear the fluty call of the loons mixed in with the sounds of the nearby greys and the periodic bleating of the foghorn down at the cape. I crawled outside the tent to pee several times that night, feeling no little anxiety to be sure, and awoke early the next morning and headed out.

Rounding the cape would undoubtedly add some new wrinkles to my paddling routine. The guide book I had along billed it as "a challenge to even the most advanced sea kayaker," which I certainly was not (a reality-check I made during more than one stretchy occasion over the next few months). As I'd heard it, a 90-foot wave had rolled past the lighthouse at Cape Scott recently (albeit in winter), and over the years a number of large ships had sunk with all hands lost. A fisherman several weeks later in Winter Harbour told me about a trawler that had gotten into trouble rounding the Cape. They had it on radar...one moment it was chugging along in mounting swell...next moment it was gone.

The Outside

As I rounded Cape Scott I experienced the damnedest juxtaposition. Sitting comfortably out on the rocks at the very northernmost tip of the island were two couples in shorts and day packs, doing lunch.

I was stunned and could not return their wave. I had put so much effort into reaching the Cape, the threshold of the most challenging phase of the journey, and here were these people that had made a laughing day-hike out of arriving at the same place.

Another hundred yards though and the hikers were forgotten.

I could see the turbulent, wave-lashed reefs that lay ahead, the large breaking waves rising up to crash over black rocks, smashing bone-white upon them. Threading my way through these tumultous seas, I had my heart in my mouth. The stretch of coastline between the tip of Vancouver Island and Winter Harbour, 40 miles south, was the most rugged of the trip. Between infrequent bays and coves, there was dear little place to come ashore in a pinch, much less to camp. I paddled into Hansen Lagoon later that day, relieved to have passed the inital challenge of the outer coast.

A Danish colony had attempted to settle Cape Scott at the turn of the century; a series of old dikes and decaying outbuilding are all that remains. At the mouth of the lagoon I tossed out a fly along the edge of a kelp bed and had a horrendous take. Slamming my rod down against the hull of the boat, the fish took one amazing surge of line and hung me up on the kelp stipes far below. I saw several salmon rolling nearby, but couldn't entice them to strike. The channel leading into the lagoon was peppered with commercial crab pots. I couldn't imagine who might be tending traps this far out, but with my own nifty break-down kayak trap I feasted on steaming dungeness crab. I found a cozy

The daily grind, prepping for Seymour Narrows. John Gornall kindly paddled out and showed me the tricks to the dangerous narrows

Fly fishing for dinner, just north of Cape Palmerston.

Black rock fish at 3 - 4 pounds.

Clearcut, Kyouquot Sound. Maximum harvest, here, right down to the water.
Forestry consciousness is rising though.

cabin after paddling a short ways up a tea-colored creek, stayed over a couple of nights, and caught some handsome cutthroat on tiny Parachute Adams.

Cape Scott is part of a huge provinical park, and the network of trails includes the beaches and coves for a good ten-mile radius. Simple, rustic cabins were scattered along the coast, especially near the park, but I seldom used them. Generally, I was happier in my tent on the beach; like a wasp's nest or a spider's web, it had assumed organic attributes after long and dependable use.

While the route due south of me was high adrenalin stuff, it was easily some of the most awesome. The big blue swells that roll south off the coast here were an extraordinary experience in a small boat. Everything seems large when you're sitting at water level. While the swells themselves were safe enough, it was where they slammed ashore or passed over reefs and sunken rocks and loomed up suddenly to break with the force of trains that made the going dicey. *But the intensity, my God!*

Late one afternoon I saw some sea critters pop up inside a kelp bed just ahead. As I paddled closer they lurched up out of the water as a group and I recognized them as sea lions. I was quite impressed, especially when they began to make threatening noises. They were suspended a good four feet out of the water, about eight of them weighing in at about a 1000 pounds per beast, when they dove in unison at me. I spun the boat on a dime and took off as fast as possible. Meanwhile, they boiled up all around my boat without ever touching it. I was relieved to make the shelter of a little bay later that afternoon. " Sea lions," I read that night, "are territorial."

I caught many black rockfish, *Sebastes melanops,* along the northwest coast. They are a fine fly-rod quarry that would take a surface troll. Many times I was struck so hard with such a powerful first run that, like a good sized mackerel, I swore I had a salmon on. They are very much a school fish and seem to hang in the kelp a lot. I would catch specimens of the same size from a given school while trolling off a bed of kelp and, if I were to pick up a five-pound rockfish, I knew I was in for some serious action.

Out on the rolling seas the next morning, I spotted a couple of shark fins cutting through the water (or so they first appeared). Ocean Sunfish, or Mola Mola, are fairly common south of the Cape. They swim on their side a lot, leaving one fin waving in the air. They resemble a large, swimming head. One baleful eye stared up at me as I paddled close to one. Eventually I tried to take one of them on a fly, and the knack to that was essentially a task of trying to drift it into its parrot-like beak. I missed, but I accidentally snagged a fin, and the surprise was that I pumped the *boat* over to the *fish,* which could have cared less, and, when I unhooked the fly, it never missed a beat.

Bear are common around much of the northern island. I would see them rummaging through piles of seaweed, picking out delicacies as they ambled along the beaches. I had to be careful to keep my food and cooking gear put away. I had one nosing around camp once, but it took off when I came out of the tent yelling. As for wolf, unfortunately I did not see one on this trip. We'd seen them before on the west coast, but this time the best I could do was to find some prints I felt pretty certain were wolf. I always had an eye out for cougars and carried a stick when I went on walks, but the most exciting encounter I had on land with an animal was when I stepped over a log on the beach one day and found a baby seal on the other side. Hissing angrily at me, it belly flopped toward the water some 20 yards away. I walked along beside it, hoping to have a moment of communion, but the little guy was quite unpleasant.

Several days later I was heading out of a fine little pocket beach in San Joseph Bay. I'd heard nothing about Cape Palmerston, jutting out into the ocean like a huge sprocket. Whereas Cape Scott was jagged, short, and sweet, Palmerston was a broad, rock-studded hemisphere and very nearly my nemesis. It had been very windy for several days out of the southeast, spelling unstable weather, and, camped where I was, I did not have a clear view of the seas off the cape. The forecast was for wind from ten to 15 knots that afternoon, along with swells of a meter or two, so I got on the water early. When I'd made it out about halfway around the Cape I noticed that both the wind and the current were stronger than I had guessed. The swells were their usual truck size, but I was expecting that; they were out of the northwest, though, and, with the wind from the other direction, they were beginning to steepen and crest.

I turned around quickly between swells and put my bow into the building sea to buy a little time and decide what to do. I knew that going back would be a long and difficult grind, but going ashore anywhere around the Cape was not much of an option either. I paddled in toward shore anyway, blindly wanting to get off the water. Angling steeply over swells, I got as close as I could to the surf line but the shore was too exposed and rocky and getting hammered by a vicious shore break. Feeling trapped, I turned around and headed back out to sea.

Panic washed over me at this point. Getting stuck out in seas that were going from bad to worse was my blackest fear. Fortunately, I came out of it fairly quickly . . . *through it* is more accurate, because it was only after I had accepted my situation that I was able to get past the fear and be able to deal.

It was unnerving having to look over my shoulder every few strokes checking for rogue waves, but the boat felt steady still, and I figured I could continue on a ways with the wind and seas astern. My obective had been Raft Cove, where, from reading the chart and factoring in prevailing current, wind, and swell, I might make it in at one spot, and one spot only, in the lee of Commerrell Point. Otherwise it looked like Waimea Bay on a good day. But that was still several miles off, and in the end that translated to several more hours.

I felt a little knot of anxiety in my gut as I made my way slowly along the coast. I had one eye peeled for any possible route ashore; occasionally I would dart in closer for a better look, but it was extremely dangerous to be paddling around this shore break. Because of a broken and rocky bottom, I could expect big waves to rise up suddenly almost anywhere. If I were to get knocked over in the surf zone, I risked being pulverized on the rocks and probably losing the boat. I turned the boat head-on into the swells for a break, rising up onto each ten-foot breast and angling steeply down the back. *Of course,* I thought in some distant part of my mind, *if things continue to worsen and darkness falls, I'll really be in a pickle.*

Once around Cape Palmerston later that afternoon though, with the squall blown over, I was feeling quite exhilarated. The seas were still huge, but that was okay; I was feeling great after having come out the back door of an old and frightening place. And *boy*, when I made it to shore that day several miles and several hours later, I was one jubilant *amigo*—happy as hell just to be ashore and sporting a new bit of *panache*.

At Winter Harbour a couple of days later, I made friends with Dick and Jane Bisset, a self-described bush couple who had migrated north a step ahead of rampant tourism in Tofino, a destination town down the coast. Dick was a master decoy carver, Jane a master sculptress. Fortunately for me, Dick was an old boatbuilder as well and generously repaired the worn spots in the hull of the Sea Lyon while Jane served us tea and lunch, a subtle

Photo by Gregg Blomberg Photography

Running hard astern. Playing a salmon in eight-to-ten foot seas was challenging. This on a three-hour open water crossing.

Photo by Gregg Blomberg Photography

Beautiful young coho about to be released.

bit of human society that I soaked up like a sponge.

I spent the afternoons working up dispatches for *Fly Rod & Reel* and the local papers at home and shopping for used paperbacks in the tiny post office along the two plank-boardwalk that fronted this quaint little fishing town. I picked up another food drop left for me by a friend who had passed through on a sailboat several weeks earlier, and before I left town four days later I was fed a marvellous prime rib dinner by a gem of a fisherman named Earl who regaled me with sea stories that nearly stood my hair on end.

Then I ran into a young guy whose dreams of adventuring were as ambitious as mine. Sam Jones III was working on an offshore albacore boat blown in by a gale. Sam described plans to roller-blade around Australia with a friend (who, as we spoke, was roller-blading across the U.S.), and I had no doubt that I'd hear an account of that trip sometime in the future. Sam also loaded me down with fresh albacore, truly the capon of the sea.

I made it all the way to the southern end of the enormous Brook's Peninsula a few days later before I was forced ashore at the very challenging Clerke Point in heavy, breaking seas (a footnote on Clerke point is that once I made Victoria I ended up on the phone with Henry Ravensdale, the canoesist who had attempted a solo circumnavigation four years earlier and who had broken up his canoe and nearly lost his life at this very same spot). There I hiked up the crystalline Clerke River near an abandoned native halibut fishing camp. Try as I might, I was unable to manifest a fish in the sweet currents of this wild and elegant stream.

Rounding the tip of the peninsula, early next morning before the sleeping giant awoke, I paddled to a secluded and deserted beach where the next day I rendezvoused with a group of my friends from home.

*World's longest hug. Meeting up with Pamela halfway around.
A very pleasant reunion.*

*Going over the charts with Gregg Blomberg. Gregg has many years
experience on Vancouver's outer coast and is highly informed as to
native cultures of the coastal Northwest.*

Photo by Author on Fujifilm

Blueback on little rod. Four-pound salmon on big dries. It doesn't get any better than this.

Photo by Author on Fujifilm

Human skull found in native burial cave. Note sugar-loaf shape from cradle board strapped to skull in infancy.

By this time I was running hard and burning lean for a guy pushing 50. Pamela couldn't believe how skinny I had gotten by the time she caught up with me. My upper body was buffed out all right, but my legs were beginning to atrophy and my ribs were showing. The group of us spent several riotous weeks together lounging on deserted beaches and fishing to schools of salmon and bottom fish. I hooked several fine, heavy coho here that had me going hard to try to keep up in the kayak. These fish would hit so hard that I could barely get the rod out of its holder because it was bent down so hard. Best of all was to find a herring ball worked into a frenzy by the salmon marauding beneath. When we'd had enough of salmon fillets and steaks, we would go after bottom fish for fish fries and *ceviche,* a delicious meal of raw cod marinated in lime juice. With a business-like 500 grain sink-tip, I hooked ling cod and a gorgeous eight-pound yellow eye in addition to plentiful quillback rock fish, and greenling. We ate our fill of fresh fish every night and never tired of it.

A series of September gales marched through at one point and pushed the waves up to the level of our tents, already pitched well back above high tideline. One look at the twisted barricade of driftwood that lay scattered even into the forest itself reminded us that this was only a summer squall compared to the nightmare winter storms. We spent the night patrolling the beach by flashlight in driving rain and had to move our tents a second time as the seas pushed wildly to the fringe of the trees.

It was the 12th of September by the time my friends headed up the long inlet where their rigs were parked. I dawdled packing up alone that morning, feeling a bit of loss about continuing on solo. Then, paddling through a cluster of islets a mile or so off the coast, I discovered a burial cave, dank and spirit-haunted and full of skulls and bones and a decomposing dugout canoe, not the type of thing to lift the spirit. Nearby I visited an abandoned, native village site with a totem pole decaying in a bed of salal. Hunkered on the gravel beach, I found a glass trade bead as a memento. The next day, just south of Rugged Point, I found a stream that meandered out of a deep cedar bog.

I paddled through tidal estuary for half a mile or so until I reached fresh water where a barricade of trees blocked my way. After wedging the long boat into the jam as far as possible, I climbed out on a half-submerged log and peered deeply down into the pool. Swimming in the dappled green waters in a shaft of light was one magnificent-looking cutthroat trout of five or so pounds. It was like an aquarium, and the trout seemed unconcerned with me. Then I noticed the leisurely rise-forms of more big trout working just upstream . . . where I could see it was impossible to get to.

I was determined, though, to try to see if I could roll a fly through the cloistered branches. I quickly strung up the three weight I'd brought along, only to discover I'd left my trout flies in camp! Not to be left untested, I unstuck the boat and paddled like hell back to camp, then turned around and paddled furiously back. I had a new problem at that point as the tide was rising steadily, and the narrow opening I had managed to slip the boat through would quickly be underwater! Still, I badly wanted to try and cover at least one of these magnificent fish. After struggling to try to get a clean presentation through a web of branches and after snagging every available one and risking getting stuck in the pool overnight, I accepted defeat and returned to camp.

As I ate breakfast the next morning I heard on my radio that two more gales would soon lash the northern coast. Rather than get pinned down on the beach with a bear that was rumored to be a bit of a rogue (we'd heard stories in the native village of Kyouquot), I opted to paddle out to a string of tiny islands riding the open ocean a mile or so offshore. I had a penchant for these little islands and would rather Crusoe my own bear-free, offshore estate than hole up on the mainland (as Vancouver Island came to feel by contrast) any day.

I had a magnificent time on Grassy Island. Built entirely out of an uplifted sedimentary bed of fossil shells, there was plenty of poking around to do between storms. During the worst of the blow I would hole up with a good book from my travelling library or work on my dispatches. If I was having trouble accessing my literary muse (common out here), all was not lost. I was carrying some extraordinary Canadian herb I'd been gifted along the way . . . there are muses, after all, and there are MUSES. The other cool thing about the island was that it had a lee shore that I could get out on, in even the worst weather. It was there in 20-knot winds, with 15 to 20-foot breakers creaming the nearby reefs that I caught a pair of fine salmon and had one brief hookup with what looked to be a big chinook.

By this time I was beginning to feel antsy about getting home before November. It was the middle of September, and I had cause for concern. Paddling the North Pacific in November was not recommended . . . October was little better. I bent to the task and by the first of October I had passed Tofino and my last food drop. Still paddling in large swell, I pushed on down the coast. Several days later I kayaked right on through the popular Broken Islands in Barkely Sound, with their designated camping sites and rangers and no shortage of signs.

On the chart, there appeared to be a passage of some kind that cut a half-circle behind the imposing promontory of Cape Beale. I made it in under a bright sun, dogging through a surf that smashed up against the cape and whooshed through the narrow channel. It was touch and go trying to get in close enough to the bluff while staying out of the break, then timing the sets and paddling with my afterburners lit to try to make it through before I was picked up in the curve of a boomer. Tied up to a concrete utility platform a little ways in, I humped the 100-odd steps up through an old-growth cedar forest to the station above.

After passing through a whitewashed gate surrounding exquisitely manicured grounds, I knocked at the door of a clean, white-washed cottage. Soon a pretty, black-haired woman greeted me with a smile and a radio stuck to one ear. Sandra Hedley held out the radio and asked me if I'd heard about the Tsunami warning:

"A Tsunami Warning is in effect. This warning is for all coastal areas and islands in the Pacific. A Tsunami has been generated which could cause damage to the coast and lands in the Pacfic. A Tsunami wave height cannot be predicted and . . . ."
Sandra said the Coast Guard had wanted to evacuate them from the lighthouse, but they'd refused. A few minutes later we could hear that the park rangers in the Broken Islands were sweeping the area to warn everyone, and apparently they were looking for me. Probably, one of the kayakers I had talked with as I was passing through had mentioned that I might be around. Sandra got on the radio and told them I was with her at the cape. We waited until 3:54, when the wave was expected. I sat out on the hundred foot bluff, watching for a giant wall of water to appear on the horizon, but it was a complete no-show. Then I spent the next day and a half waiting for the seas to settle down enough for me to make it out the southern opening in the channel without losing control of my sphincter.

Finally, I got up the nerve to shoot the works. I busted out through a wild line of breaking combers and hung a hard left. Two minutes of heartfelt stroking later I was home free! It had even been pleasantly exciting to watch the waves rise up from rolling swells like great sea moles coming out of their holes and

The versatile Frisbee serves as both plate and recreation. Disk heaven here, rolling out of our tents to hot sun, warm sand, pot of coffee. Sprinting on the beach and playing catch. Then diving in the surf to cool off.

Travelling with the fleet. Heading south again for a couple of days, camping on little islands along the way.

explode all around me, *but without the sound track.* I had stuck in a couple of earplugs just before launching, after I realized that it was the *noise* of the booming waves that unglued me most!

That evening, several miles down the coast, I was camped along a shallow bay fixing dinner when I noticed some activity on the water. Looking closely, I could make out the rise-forms and splashes of fish feeding at the surface! I quickly strung up the little rod, tied on a size #6 Stimulator, and tossed it out.

Boom . . . a hefty, mint-bright salmon came skyrocketing out of the bay, took line aggressively in surges and jumped repeatedly before I could slide it upon the gravel beach. It was a gorgeous four-pound fish.

I could hardly contain my enthusiasm for the next hour as I caught and released half a dozen strong young coho, or "bluebacks" as the Canadians call them, because of a cerulean blue coloring to the dorsal surface. I never did figure out exactly what they were feeding on . . . fry or shrimp or krill, maybe, scattered at the surface. They liked my fly, though, fished like a noisy dry during a stonefly hatch. The harder I slammed it on the surface, the more it interested them. When I skittered it toward shore, they would chase after it half out of the water! I felt like I was back on the Deschutes casting to big redsides gorging on salmonflies.

Next morning there were still some fish around, so I lingered packing up, taking some time to enjoy fishing drys in the salt, a strange and exquisite experience. But it was October now, with squalls and gales on the way to usher in winter, and my son was already well into his football season at home. The reality of running late in the season, with little means for catching up, was sinking in.

I had once hiked the stretch of coastline that I paddled along for the next couple of days. The West Coast Trail is a lifesaving link in Canada's grim history of shipwrecks along this stretch of coast. After the wreck of the Valencia in 1906 and the death of all 126 survivors, the lifesaving route to civilization was finally established.

I passed Tsusiat Falls that crashes into the sea near the native village of Clo-ose and ended up surfing ashore within spitting distance of a park crew spike camp working on nearby trails. I was pretty hungry for some human interaction again by then, and the crew of Fleming, Malcolm, Dan and Terry graciously invited me into their wall-tent for a delicious dinner. We convened again in the predawn hours for a hugillous breakfast. To top that, the fellows loaded me down with steaks, chicken, chops, and coffee that morning as I was packing up. I screwed the pooch on my first attempt at leaving the beach and got banged up by the boat swinging around wildly in the soup. Big shore-breaks were the worst, and this one easily qualified. Fleming ran over and stabilized the boat for me, and next try I was climbing toward the moon, hoping the huge wave wouldn't break before I punched through.

From there it was a several-day layover at the Carmanah lighthouse's empty, Coast Guard cabin to dodge a bit of weather, and a Canadian thanksgiving dinner with the very hospitable keeper, Jerry, his wife Janet, and their children, Jake and Justine. In return I taught them Horse and Around the World on their cliff-top basketball court. Cause for celebration here for me as well—the Carmanah Light marks the entrance proper to the Strait of Juan de Fuca, the broad channel that leads like a cervix into the womb of Puget Sound and my little cluster of home islands nestled there like eggs.

A few days later I was down coast another 20 miles, pitching camp in a hotel room in Port Renfrew, courtesy of Maureen and Rick, the proprietors. The hotel is vintage turn of the century, rustic and clean, and the rooms are finished in a rich chocolate-brown lath. I holed up in the bridal suite (sans bride) that night, sneaked in a Mr. Coffee brewer from the hall, and heated up a can of Irish stew on the burner. Leaving port the next morning, I buckled down to the business of getting home. In reality, there was little more to do to speed my return than I was doing. The *buckling down* and *bending to it* business was mostly psychological, to get me up an hour earlier, dawdle a little less, and maybe stay on the water an hour longer each day. As for speed, other than the sail on windy days, it was just a matter of sticking in the saddle.

I made Sombrio Beach late that afternoon (haven for surfers and squatters), secured camp and walked down the beach to check out the scene. As luck would have it, I'd trolled through a school of big blacks on my way south and carried one with me now on a stick. At what looked like the flagship of the community, a verandaed, two-story driftwood cabin with a yard and a flagpole, I walked up to two fellows sitting on the porch. One of them called out with a grin, "Walk softly and carry a big fish, eh? There's a policy!" We all laughed at this, and I listened as the men narrated the 20-year history of the settlement of squatters there. South of Sombrio, wildness deteriorated rapidly.

Pushing south to yet another refuge at the lighthouse on Trial Island, I passed Victoria and a graffati-ravaged sea wall (my favorite was the $ symbol with an X through it—graffiti haiku). From there I had been considering a straight-shot crossing of the Strait to Cattle Pass and home, but, upon closer inspection of the map (as well as direct eyeballing of one yawning amount of open water . . . 18 to 20 miles), I decided that circuity was the better part of valor. It might take me two extra days to get around by rounding Victoria and island-hopping home, but hey . . . better late than never.

Annie Brooks checking the smoke house. Scavenged from driftwood and chinked with seaweed, it did a credible job of smoking our plentiful fresh salmon.

Friends from home, keeping themselves amused. These guys are jugglers too.

Mola Mola swimming on its side. They range to several hundred pounds and resemble a swimming head.

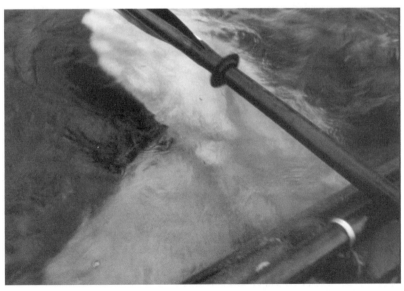

Mola Mola, or Ocean Sunfish, about to 'catch and release.'

I rang up Bob Tyrell of Orca Books on the radio phone as I paddled from Trial Island. We would meet at an upscale marina not far ahead. Although Bob had published *Rivers of Dreams,* a collecton of fly fishing stories I'd put together a couple of years back, we had never met in person.

The weather was cold and blustery as I sailed into the marina. With bare feet and my raunchy wet suit still on, I must have looked (and smelled) curiously out of place in the chic cafe as Bob graciously bought one broke and hungry sailor lunch. As I prepared to push off into the teeth of a squall, Bob generously loaded me up with bagels, pears, and brie, and plenty of strong Canadian beer . . . a very welcome bit of *bon voyage.*

While I was pinned down in a little bay below a subdivision at Gordon Head the next day, a gentleman walking the beach stopped and invited me to dinner. Mark Gruber works as an environmental attorney in the metropolis behind the beach, and so during my final evening in British Columbia I had a refreshing meal of macaroni and cheese with his children and a gorgeous foreign exchange student. Mark put me on track with some of the long-needed environmental changes underway in the province. I had talked with a number of locals along the way and experienced first-hand the obscene clear-cuts and the subsequent damage to the watersheds and the adverse trickle-down effects that destroyed many of the native salmon and steehead runs that were once a legacy of this remarkable island. Dave and Rory, Dick and Jane, Earl, and many others . . . everyone seemed to have a handle on what was happening.

The thing about these B.C. temperate rainforests, Mark explained that night, is that, besides being simply an awesome place, they support one of the largest and most diverse ecosystems in the world. To reduce these marvellous organic palaces to stumps to satisfy the greed of the logging industry is a heinous thing.

While someone will have to bite the bullet if real changes are to be effected in time, it sounded like as much as possible was being done to protect the livlehood of the logging communties that would be hardest hit. Stumpage fees had been raised, and, charging more per tree, meant less harvest and more money to put these same men and women to work with watershed restoration, road rehab, silviculture and other conservation projects. Word was there would be a 25-to-35-percent increase in protected forest as a result of the recent Forests Practices Code Act. I got a recent comparison study in the mail when I returned home and discovered that, although the new legislation is certainly a step in the right direction, the B.C. regulations that are self-touted as "world class" fall short of our own standards here in Washington state in *eight* out of *ten* categories. Robert Kennedy Jr., who prefaced the report, summed up the situation: "There is a long way to go to implement ecologically sound management in the ancient forests that straddle the Canada-U.S. Border." And wise management of our shared forest resources, of course, spells wise management of remaining native steelhead and salmon stocks.

After a long and exciting crossing of windswept Haro Strait and a near circumnavigation of San Juan Island in the process, I surfed ashore in a nasty four-foot chop onto the spit along Fisherman's Bay where I had launched from, over a quarter of a year earlier. I had been unable to make radio contact with a marine operator coming down the east coast of San Juan Island; consequently, Pamela had no idea when I would be arriving. There was no one there to greet me on the beach that evening, much less drive me home in the gathering dark. I had one last beer in the boat, however, and dug around to find it. Still in my stinking, torn wet suit, with rain clouds scudding overhead and darkness about to descend, I collapsed on the beach, leaned back aganst a driftwood log, and drank it down.

God, it was good to be home.

Fishermen Who Paddle With the Whales

One of the ironies of travelling alone is that it's just more likely to turn out to be a social experience. All along the way I encountered extraordinary men and women in the fish camps and ports, many of whom I have mentioned already, most of whom I haven't. Some of them were fisheries people on the water or parks people or lighthouse keepers or the Coast Guard. I was given lifts by them, fed by them, and generally nourished and kept an eye on by these big-hearted people. I had the feeling they shared my own dream in some way and saw a part of themselves in me. I met a Catholic missionary who served the native villages along the outer coast and travelled back and forth in a little double-end Columbia bar dory called the Smiley and who gave me a much needed lift around Estevan Point. I met Shawn Selongosky, builder and proprietor of The Ark at Hot Springs Cove and a man who inspired me deeply; Shawn fed me and offered me the deck of his floating B&B to make repairs on the Sea Lyon. I was taken in by the lighthouse keepers along the coast who shared their headland homes with me when I was running through the gales of October. For a guy that was travelling solo, I had more re-affirming and inspirational encounters with people than I could have possibly imagined.

This voyage contained more than a few dangerous moments for me, much as I had expected, but it was not a devil-may-care attitude I carried with me that summer. Nor was it the junkie's search for the Adrenaline God. Rather, it was quite simply a sustained opportunity to live in a sacred state of adventure and to receive everything that such an experience has to offer. It's good to be tested every once in a while, I believe, to put our life on the line and see what we've got to work with—something we've gone out of our way as a culture to avoid.

A special thanks to Ken Morrish, Jeffrey Stonehill, and the Sierra Club of Western Canada (my sole financial backers), and to my partner, Pamela Maresten, who mailed food packages to points along my route, sent me money when I ran out, and supported my journey most fundamentally of all. And finally, a 'thank you' to Jim Kakuk of Tsunami. Quite simply, the boat did everything he had said it would.

Sponsors and support from:

Aaron Reels
Action Optics
Adventure Foods
Body Glove
Cortland
Coleman
Downeast Sportscraft
Eastaboga Tackle
Extrasport
Fly Rod & Reel
Glaciar Glove
Hexagraph Rods
Icom
Just Good Foods
Katadyn
Krieger
Leica
Mackenzie Anglers
Magellan
Management by Intuition

Moonstone
Ortlieb
Outdoor Research
Patagonia
Pelican
Petzyl
PMI
PowerBar
Primex
Sawyer
Sierra Club of W. Canada
SPORTea
Spyderco
SportsTech
SSA
Stowaway
Treo
Tsunami
Wyoming Woolens

ORDER FORM

WATER MARKED

Journal of a Naked Fly Fisherman

by ROBERT LYON

TO ORDER:

By Phone or Fax: 360-468-3250

Via Internet: lyon@interisland.net • www.interisland/net

By mail: Fill out the form below and send with your remittance to:
Water Marked Press
4161 Lopez Sound Road, Lopez, WA 98261

Name..

Address..

City...

State and Zip..

Daytime Phone...

Visa or Mastercard Number...Exp. Date..........

Name on Card...

Signature..

Price per book: $18.95 U.S. $29.60 CAN
Shipping & Handling: $3 first book, add $1 for each additional book.

Washington residents add 7.7% sales tax.

Total enclosed...